THE EARLY COMMUNITY
AT BEDFORD PARK

THE EARLY COMMUNITY
AT BEDFORD PARK

"CORPORATE HAPPINESS"
IN THE FIRST GARDEN SUBURB

by Margaret Jones Bolsterli

ROUTLEDGE & KEGAN PAUL

LONDON AND HENLEY

First published in Great Britain in 1977
by Routledge & Kegan Paul Ltd
39 Store Street,
London WC1E 7DD and
Broadway House,
Newtown Road,
Henley-on-Thames,
Oxon RG9 1EN

Printed in the United States of America

British Library Cataloguing in Publication Data

Bolsterli, Margaret Jones
    The early community at Bedford Park.
    1. Bedford Park, London — Social life and
    customs
    I. Title
    942.1'82   DA685.B/   76-8299

    ISBN 0-7100-8693-8

FOR DAVID AND ERIC AND BETHANY

CONTENTS

ILLUSTRATIONS

ACKNOWLEDGMENTS

It gives me great pleasure to thank the many people who have helped and encouraged me in this project. I am especially indebted to Professor G. Robert Stange for introducing me to Bedford Park in the first place and to T. A. Greeves who gave me insight into the peculiar spirit of Bedford Park. Professor Bethany K. Dumas gave invaluable advice after reading the manuscript in its various stages of development. My sons were always sympathetic and encouraging. Professors Mort Karp and Martha Dellinger were most helpful with suggestions for the manuscript in its final form. Martha Dellinger and Randy Murphy helped with the art work.

I thank the National Endowment for the Humanities for the Younger Humanist Grant which enabled me to spend a year in London to do the research, and I am grateful to the University of Arkansas for a year's leave from teaching to do the research and writing.

Libraries which extended courtesy and help to me were the London Borough of Hounslow Library Services: Chiswick District Library, Columbia University Libraries, the Royal Institute of British Architects, and the British Museum. Miss Winifred Heard, reference librarian of the Chiswick District Library, merits special recognition for her kindness as well as for her help. I am indebted to the London Borough of Hounslow and the Chiswick District Library for permission to use a photograph of the plan of Bedford Park and to Columbia University Libraries for permission to reproduce four photographs and a letter from the Moncure Conway Collection.

Parts of chapters 1 and 4 have appeared in different form in *Centennial Review* and *Michigan Papers in Women's Studies*.

INTRODUCTION

The Suburban Impulse

It has always seemed to me that the most fruitful areas in cultural history are the turning points, those periods of transition from one phase of society to another, the times when one can see shifts in attitudes. Perhaps the most obvious of these, because it is still in process in late twentieth century, is the shift from Victorian to Modern. These labels have meaning to the extent that one can refer to Victorian or Modern ideas about furniture, houses, sex, the novel, poetry, or clothes with the knowledge that a difference is implied. But the problem gets more complicated, and therefore more interesting to the cultural historian, when it comes to something as basic to the twentieth-century vision of the shape of life as the suburban community. This vision, advertised in every newspaper in America as a *community*, usually has a shopping center, social center, church, and houses on individual plots built according to slightly differing specifications to conform to some sort of master plan with architectural integrity. These developments ring every city and town of medium size, and, in fact, the dream is so pervasive that it is no longer confined to suburbs. Well-to-do farmers in the Middle West and the South live in communities built on this same pattern from which they commute to their farms and small towns in those areas have come to serve the same function as suburbs around cities. The dream of life in these "subruran" communities is the same as it is in the suburban ones: the vision has become identified with a way of life, not with escape from urban living. Where did the transition come between the Victorian concept of a suburb as a conglomeration of rowhouses and the Modern concept as an integral community? Early experiments like Hampstead Garden Suburb and the new towns of Welwyn and Letchworth seem too comprehensive. There must have been an intermediate step.

Several years ago while doing some work on the Aesthetic Movement and the poet William Butler Yeats I was surprised to find that Bedford Park, the community of "artistic crackpots" in which Yeats's father, the painter John Butler Yeats, lived among numerous friends during the last quarter of the nineteenth century, bore a striking resemblance to the suburban communities advertised by progressive builders today. Could it be possible, I wondered, that here in this tiny colony, described by its founders to be utopian in nature, lay one of those turning points where the shift in values from Victorian to Modern involved something so vast and important as the shift from a dream of the good life applicable to a few Victorians to the dominant shape of life in the twentieth century. It seemed farfetched, on the face of it, to look for a connection between the sophisticated community which appealed to those Aesthetes in 1876 and communities which appeal to Modern people from all walks of life. The one common element seemed to be a dream of community. I spent a year in England studying Victorian accounts of the founding of Bedford Park, talking to elderly people who grew up there (as well as to more recent local residents who still claim for the place a sense of community unlike any other in London), and examining the community which remains today. It is my conclusion that the dream at work in the early days of Bedford Park was the genesis of the modern dream of the suburban community. This is not to claim lineal descent; cultural history consists of a sequence of responses to technological events, and the development of the suburb lies in the refinement of the suburban dream to match advancing sophistication in methods of transportation. The dream is the same whether one traveled to it by commuter train in 1876 or by Chevrolet in 1976. This study is an exploration of the early phase of that dream.

Bedford Park was such an isolated phenomenon in its time that it is tempting to discuss it in isolation. But to take it out of context is to destroy its historical place as part of the suburban impulse of the nineteenth century; looked at in retrospect it was a logical step in a long sequence of events.

There seem to be two principles behind the impulse to move to the suburbs: escape from urban problems and a search for a new life style. While the effort to escape is usually the most urgent (people have always wanted improved sanitary conditions, more space, clean air, and better conditions for raising families), the search for a new style of living outside the limitations of city life is also a strong pull to the suburbs. Lewis Mumford notes in *The City in History* that the original creators of the suburb were looking for a place where their private fantasies could be expressed without sacrificing the privileges and benefits of urban life.[1] Suburbs became visible almost as early as the city itself, yet their peculiar situation of dependency on the city seems to have kept them from being taken seriously until fairly recently. Their growth since 1800, of course, has been phenomenal, but they have been in existence in one form or another since prebiblical times. To understand the evolution of the modern suburb it is necessary to understand the dual nature of the suburban impulse, because the suburb which offers only escape is more likely to become, in its turn, another slum than the one which offers a dream of community and a shape of life different from that offered by the city.

The economic pull to the cities which turned English society from an agrarian to an urban one in the nineteenth century was balanced by a pull back toward rural areas which dumped people in suburbs that were as ill equipped to provide for them as the cities were. Moving to the suburbs was no solution to urban problems, for most suburban dwellers had to contend with what had been similar urban problems of overcrowding, jerry-built houses, and poor sanitation as well as those problems endemic to suburbs: boredom, the sterility of a new environment, and problems of deracination (those of finding a sense of community among people without a common background). It was Bedford Park's solution to these social problems that marked its unique quality as a suburban community.

If a need to escape urban problems is the primary force at work in the attraction to the suburbs, the facts of urban growth in Britain between 1800 and 1900 are impressive enough to explain that need, and London, of course, was at the forefront of the massive move to the cities. In 1801, 20 percent of the population of England and Wales lived in cities with 10,000 or more inhabitants. By 1851, the number had grown to 38 percent. The 1851 census recorded for the first time that the aggregate urban population exceeded the rural population, if only by a margin of less than one percentage point.[2] As for London, it grew from just under a million inhabitants in 1801 to four and a half million in 1901, by which time it contained 20 percent of the entire population of England and Wales.[3] To a utilitarian like Dickens's Mr. Gradgrind, these staggering figures might be enough to explain the urban problem, but, overwhelming as they are, facts do not tell the whole story, for they do not measure the human factor, and misery is qualitative as well as quantitative. The modern imagination which has not had to deal with the physical facts of unpaved streets, of air clogged with soft coal smoke from household fires as well as from industrial chimneys, or with the problems of housing millions of people in spaces that could not be expanded to meet their needs, may benefit from the descriptions of London given by eyewitnesses. Charles Dickens began *Bleak House* this way:

> London. Michaelmas Term lately over, and the Lord Chancellor sitting in Lincoln's Hall. Implacable November weather. As much mud in the streets as if the waters had but newly retired from the face of the earth, and it would not be wonderful to meet a megalosaurus, forty feet long or so, waddling like an elephantine lizard up Holborn Hill. Smoke lowering down from chimney pots, making a soft black drizzle, with flakes of soot in it as big as full-grown snow flakes—gone into mourning, one might imagine, for the death of the sun. Dogs, undistinguishable in mire. Horses, scarcely better, splashed to their very blinkers. Foot passengers, jostling one another's umbrellas, in a general infection of ill-temper, and losing their foothold at street-corners, where tens of thousands of other foot passengers have been slipping and sliding since the day broke (if this day ever broke) adding new deposits to the crust upon crust of mud, sticking at those points tenaciously to the pavement, and accumulating at compound interest.
>
> Fog everywhere. Fog up the river, where it flows among green aits and meadows; fog down the river, where it rolls defiled among the tiers of shipping, and the waterside pollutions of a great (and dirty) city.[4]

This is a *public* London scene, an experience in which everyone from highest to lowest classes participated. It might not have been enough to drive people out of the city if they had been able to escape it to comfortable private surroundings, to homes built to fit their needs and dreams. The notion that this might have been the case is discredited by the account of another eyewitness, H. G. Wells, who described the houses people had to live in as matching Dickens's grim street scene quoted above.

> Once they were erected there was no getting rid of these ugly dingy pretentious substitutes for civilized housing. They occupied the ground. There was no choice; people had to do with them and pay the high rents demanded. . . . To most Londoners of my generation those row and jerry-built unalterable homes seemed to be as much in the nature of things as rain in September and it is only with the wisdom of retrospect, that I realize the complete irrational scrambling planlessness of which all of us who had to live in London were the victims. . . . Each house had an ill-lit basement with kitchen, coal cellars and so forth below ground level. Above this was the dining-room and a bureau; above this again was a drawing-room and above this a floor or so of bedrooms in diminishing scale. No bathroom was provided and at first the plumbing was of a very primitive kind. . . . most things, coals, slops, and so forth had to be carried by hand up and down the one staircase. This was the London house, that bed of Procrustes to which the main masses of accumulating population of the most swiftly growing city of the world . . . everyone indeed who ranked between the prosperous householder and the slum denizen had to fit their lives. The multiplying multitudes poured into these moulds with no chance of protest or escape.[5]

What could be more natural than to dream of escaping this squalor by moving to the edge of the city into new developments of new houses where the air, theoretically, was cleaner, and the houses not permeated with the stale aura of previous generations? One problem with this dream was that after 1830 or so advances in methods of transportation made it too easy to be realized. The air *was* better on the outskirts of the city, and frequently sanitation was better in new houses; but the popularity of the escape fantasy was frequently that dream's undoing. The headlong rush of speculative developers to meet the demands of commuters led to mile after mile of identical suburban houses offering little better accommodation than the houses of Wells's youth. The closely built-up suburbs like Camberwell and Hornsey with their miles of row houses may have been an improvement in terms of density, but their sterility still left a blank in the actual lives of people. Beyond these there were indeed outer suburbs with individual houses on their own plots of ground, but even if one had successfully escaped the city and found the ideal little miniature castle or villa, only half of the suburban fantasy would have been met, for the sense of community was still missing. The people who had left the inhuman city frequently found themselves in the dehumanized world of a sterile suburb. Furthermore, one day's suburb often became the next day's slum as the search led the affluent further and further out and the less affluent followed as far as they could. So much for the escape side of the suburban coin.

The answers to the discovery side of the suburban problem are complicated by the state of community planning in Victorian England, which not only was minimal but confined to attempts to provide relief for the working class while the move to the suburbs was predominantly a middle-class phenomenon. The model factory villages of the north, like Saltaire and Ackroyden, are examples of a paternalistic attempt to relieve the misery caused by industrialization and consequent urbanization. Built by factory owners to provide housing for workers in cloth mills, they were a part of the aura of utopian reform theories current throughout the century, but it is interesting that the utopias were primarily working-class utopias. Middle-class utopias were not part of the scheme; the middle classes were expected to fend for themselves. Bedford Park, the first middle-class attempt to use theories of cooperation and planning that had been worked out for the relief of the working classes, bears a striking resemblance to the pattern of those model villages, for, while it was not paternalistic, it had a patriarch, and the basis of the early community was the spirit of cooperation long associated with working-class efforts to organize political and economic means to make community life easier. However, in spite of the use of these theories, Bedford Park was founded as and remained that strange and unusual phenomenon, a middle-class utopia.

Chapter 1

BACKGROUND

In 1876 a speculative builder named Jonathan Thomas Carr began building a housing estate, Bedford Park, adjoining the Turnham Green Station of the Metropolitan Railway Line on the western edge of London. (Fig. 1) The community which evolved in this housing estate was unique and successful in so many ways that people flocked to live in it; its developments and activities were closely followed by the contemporary press; and it has recently been the subject of serious study by an architect interested in town planning, a literary historian, an art historian, and a practicing architect.[1] It has been characterized by Sir John Betjeman as "the most significant suburb built in the last century, probably in the western world."[2]

Bedford Park is interesting extrinsically for its position in cultural history and intrinsically for the quality of life produced there. It was the first garden suburb, for it was not until 1892, with *Garden Cities of Tomorrow*, that Ebenezer Howard introduced the idea of the garden city, an extension, according to Betjeman, of the Bedford Park experiment. Letchworth was begun in 1903, Hampstead Garden Suburb in 1907, and Welwyn Garden City in 1919. There had not been an attempt, before Bedford Park, to provide a self-contained community of comfortable, moderately priced yet attractive houses for the middle classes.

Efforts had been made in isolated cases to provide for the working classes, for example, in the paternalistic factory villages of the north like Saltaire, begun in 1850 by Sir Titus Salt. And there were middle-class suburbs, of course, before 1876. But none offered the features of Bedford Park, for it was complete with church, stores, club, and tavern, and it was designed to offer a wide variety of choice in house design within the basic unity of one architectural style, Queen Anne Revival. The usual suburb was monotonous in appearance and dull to live in; Bedford Park was interesting to look at and apparently fascinating to live in. It was unique in its attraction for a large number of creative people and in its combination of life and art. It was a community attuned to the art of living, a fact which proved to be the downfall of some of its artists who found the life it provided too pleasant to bother themselves with art.

The elements which conspired to make Bedford Park an immediate success are among the reasons why it is so important in cultural history. It had the special appeal of an architectural and social experiment. Walter Creese's term for it as an "oasis" in his study, *The Search for Environment*, is descriptive of some of this appeal, but there were elements other than the desire to escape the monotony of the urban and suburban deserts that made it a success. It was an experiment whose time had come; for one thing, it was precisely the time for the Queen Anne Revival style of architecture to appeal to a certain type of resident. It was also precisely the time for a community with a slight flavor of Aestheticism to appeal to those residents, and it was the right time for a group of people interested in community to come together and form one on the basis of their common interests. Although it was not by any means socialistic, Bedford Park was able to draw on the theories of the cooperative movement that were so popular in nineteenth-century thought and modify them for its practical needs. It was, perhaps, the only time in history when those common interests could be focused on art in a middle-class neighborhood so that the architectural experiment reinforced the social experiment. Finally, it was a lucky coincidence that the man who founded Bedford Park was interested in building a community in which he would like to live and raise his own family. This meant that while it was a speculative venture it was not made primarily for financial gain; it was a speculative venture into a new kind of community and a new way of life. These were the cohesive forces that produced a functioning community and fostered the foundation of social organizations which outlasted the original ideals of the community by many years.

Bedford Park is significant in cultural history also because it illustrates one of those moments in time when a major shift can be observed in an art form and a social organization. This shift in an art form was one in architectural style from Victorian revivalism to modern functionalism, and it began at Bedford Park first of all in the use of Queen Anne Revival, which in its infinite possibilities for variety was really internally functional while it retained the external characteristics of an identifiable revival style. The shift can be explained in this way: modern architectural design works from the inside to the outside of a house; the design of a house today is expected to fit the needs of the people who are going to live in it. External appearance is subordinated to this internal function; it does not have to conform to a notion of style based on the appearance of another house. But before the flexibility of the Queen Anne style was demonstrated at Bedford Park, houses tended to be designed from the outside in, because they were expected to conform to a preconceived notion of style. People were poured into whatever shape the house

11

took. Queen Anne Revival, with its loose eclecticism, was an intermediate step between the rigidity of Gothic and Palladian styles and truly functional design which is "no-style," strictly speaking, because no functional house is expected to resemble a model. Bedford Park is a textbook example of the capabilities of Queen Anne, because people for whom the houses were designed were allowed to make requests about specifications. Basic designs provided by the architects could be varied almost infinitely by the builders to suit clients and yet retain the architectural integrity of the area. In 1876 it was still necessary to build in some recognizable revival style, but the flexibility of Queen Anne made it the last gasp of serious revivalism. Once the desirability of this flexible approach had been demonstrated, it was no longer necessary to support revivalism.

Socially, Bedford Park was an experiment in what might be called "capitalistic communal" living, in that while many of the residents were interested in sharing public facilities and enterprises, they were not ready to sacrifice the privacy of individual homes. For example, at one time they considered having a communal kitchen, but not communal meals; provisions were to be made for hot dinners to be delivered to separate houses at mealtime. This community was an experiment in cooperation without the rigid theory one might expect to underlie the institutions, for the institutions were pragmatic, growing out of needs as they arose. Despite an occasional bitter fight, the community functioned for several years with a surprising amount of harmony, but by the late 1880s the cohesive forces were disintegrating for reasons I shall develop in the following chapters. The shift from Victorian to Modern had obviously begun, and the ideal of that type of community is still being offered by every developer who throws in the lure of a country club to attract people to his development. The present equivalent of that architectural experiment where houses are similar enough for a kind of unity yet varied enough to interest the eye can be seen in the many different types of ranch houses available in any suburban tract in America where the builder has taken the trouble to try to avoid monotony. The contemporary suburb is usually an extension of the experiment at Bedford Park and those where the builder has tried to foster some kind of *social* success like that achieved at Bedford Park, Reston in Virginia and New Ash Green in England, for example, have found themselves facing the same problems: how to plan a community which can be cohesive through common interests of the residents and yet appeal to people in different age groups and income levels, and how to make a financial as well as social success.

Writers for the architectural press were intrigued by the events surrounding the foundation of Bedford Park and followed the plans and construction there in great detail. Sometimes it was a matter of outraged interest, but there was never any doubt that it was a venture worth following. While the architectural innovations were worthy of public note, social innovations were equally as interesting, and the modern reader is fortunate that Bedford Park had both a historian and a chronicle. The historian was Moncure Conway, the American Unitarian minister and journalist who had a missionary's zeal to convert the rest of the world to the Bedford Park way of life. The chronicle was *The Bedford Park Gazette*, published monthly from July 1883, until July 1884. Like the medieval chroniclers who started their histories of England with the Trojan War, H. R. Fox Bourne, the editor of the *Gazette*, began his first issue with a retrospective account of the foundation of the community before limiting the intent of his paper to monthly record and calendar. His stated intention was to

13

keep the paper objective; a calendar of coming events, reports on past events, and railway timetables were to be the contents. However, after the first issue he was entreated to become the critic of the community. While declining to do this, he proposed instead to print a column of criticism by an Outsider who could be objective and yet avoid the pillory by his anonymity. Since the Outsider knew so much about Bedford Park it is obvious that he was very much an insider and was probably Fox Bourne himself. At any rate, his columns and the outraged letters to the editor which they evoked are a fine source of information about the community. It is worth noting that in spite of the statement of editorial objectivity at the beginning, the editor was openly taking sides in public disputes by the end of the year. He was, after all, one of the more active members of the community. The hopes that were rampant in 1883 and 1884 for a new kind of community were reflected in this little paper which was intended, as the editor claimed, to be a "fair and comprehensive reflex of life in Bedford Park,"[3] and its demise after only a year of publication was part of the first real crisis of the community.

The Bedford Park Gazette was a "company" paper, in some respects, edited by a believer in the community who was willing to defend it in general while occasionally criticizing particular faults with an eye to their remedy. *The Action, Chiswick, & Turnham Green Gazette* had a different aim in reporting whatever was interesting both to residents of Bedford Park and their neighbors in surrounding areas. There was a running commentary in both editorial and news columns from the very beginning including, on occasion, details of committee meetings, parties, dramatic performances, and church ritual. In addition to this local coverage there were occasional articles about the activities in Bedford Park in London papers. Bedford Park was news in those days because of its architectural interest and its community—the same interests which it holds for the historian.

Other valuable information comes from the memoirs of people like G. K. Chesterton and William Butler Yeats who knew the place when they were young men and reflected on it later in their autobiographies. Yeats's father, John Butler Yeats, moved his family to Bedford Park on two different occasions. Bedford Park is also the Saffron Park of Chesterton's novel, *The Man Who Was Thursday*, and the Biggleswick of John Buchan's *Mr. Standfast*. But the most important source is the work of Moncure Daniel Conway, whose accounts for *Harper's Magazine* and later reflections in his autobiography permeate all subsequent accounts. He was there, he knew what the aims of Bedford Park were, and he approved so thoroughly that he wanted to tell the world all about it. He was a man of varied interests, an authority on demonology, a literary critic whose special interest was the work of Nathaniel Hawthorne, and an expert at billiards (a game which he learned from John Bright and Peter Taylor). It was said of him that his coat of arms should be a pulpit impaled on a billiard cue. He was a catch for Bedford Park because he knew so many people and was so active in pursuing his double career. Next to Jonathan Carr he was probably the most influential man in the park from his arrival in 1880 until 1884 when he moved his family to New York. His account of his first acquaintance with Bedford Park and his subsequent removal there indicates some of the appeal of the place. In an article in *Harper's New Monthly Magazine* Conway relates that one day, after an absence of five years, he happened to be near Chiswick and decided to have a look at the field where Prince Rupert and his Cavaliers had camped in retreat from the Roundheads, a field which had

15

more recently been made into a botanical garden by the horticulturist, Joseph Lindley. To his astonishment there was a picturesque village where he had expected only fruit trees, vegetables, and flowers. (See figs. 2 and 3) The trees still stood, but houses had been built among them in a style which made the village appear "aged" although he knew it to be less than five years old. He remarks that they are "aesthetic" houses which "differed from each other sympathetically, in pleasing competition as to which could be prettiest."[4] He was so enchanted that within a year he was living in Bedford Park, in a house designed and built to fit the needs and taste of his family. The visual appeal was only one of the reasons the Conways decided to move to Bedford Park. Two other compelling reasons were the quality of life offered by the community, and, equally as important for a minister who had to supplement his income with journalism, economy. The following excerpt of a letter from Mrs. Conway spells out the financial advantage of the move.

> . . . A friend of ours offers to build us a house on part of his estate (where he has formed a little colony) opposite his own house. He will build according to our wishes (within certain limits) a house consisting of Drawing room, Dining room, Billiard room, Study, 7 bedrooms, box room, kitchen, scullery, larder, cellars & closets, balcony roof with railing around it over the kitchen: ground 100 ft. front 120 deep for £1500, ground rent of £24 per year. This would be for 99 years not freehold. We are paying now £174 per year & £48 taxes and he will I fear compel us to make repairs through some misunderstanding. Our taxes will be only about £18.[5]

This house, called Inglenook after the Conway estate in Virginia, may be seen in figure 4.

In his account for *Harper's*, Conway goes on to define the appeal of Bedford Park by explaining the predicament

of people who were not wealthy but who had been educated to appreciate beauty in houses and decorations.
Where were they to live? It was prohibitively expensive to
have a house which deviated from the "normal" style unless
one were a millionaire or an artist who could do the work
himself. No one else could afford any variation from the
conventional decoration. His use of the term "aesthetic"
for the houses in Bedford Park is a tip to what he meant
by deviation from the normal, for *aesthetic* was synonymous
with *artistic* and *Queen Anne* when used as a term in architecture and decorating. Technically, Queen Anne Revival
was a non-Gothic, non-Palladian style of limited eclecticism employing different combinations of the following
vocabulary: red brick exterior; tall sash windows which
may be surmounted with a segmental arch containing a
brick keystone, this arch often surmounted by a brick mold-
ing following the curvature; white window and door frames;
gables, sometimes curved and shaped in the Dutch manner,
sometimes straight; tall chimneys; and the sunflower motif
stamped anywhere there was appropriate space for it.[6]
The style probably became associated with artists and
Aestheticism through the architects E. W. Godwin and
Norman Shaw who designed houses for artists and were,
of course, the first two architects employed at Bedford
Park. It was possible to build cheaply in the Queen Anne
style, and, since it offered almost infinite possibilities of
variation, it was possible to achieve that deviation from
the "normal" which attracted Conway. Shaw's houses at
Bedford Park went a long way toward cementing the re-
lationship between *Aesthetic*, *artistic*, and *Queen Anne*.
Aesthetic interior decoration leaned toward dull, even sub-
dued colors and light furniture. The ultimate in Aesthetic
elegance was probably achieved in the houses decorated
by E. W. Godwin for James McNeill Whistler and Oscar

Wilde. William Butler Yeats's description of Wilde's house shows, perhaps, an extreme of "Aesthetic decoration which stands in the highest contrast to the ordinary Victorian taste for mahogany and patterns."

> He lived in a little house at Chelsea that the architect Godwin had decorated with an elegance that owed something to Whistler. There was nothing medieval nor pre-Raphaelite, no cupboard door with figures upon flat gold, no peacock blue, no dark background. I remember vaguely a little drawing room with Whistler etchings "let in" to white panels, and dining-room all white, chairs, walls, mantelpiece, carpet, except for a diamond-shaped piece of red cloth in the middle of the table under a terra-cotta statuette. It was perhaps too perfect in its unity.[7]

The decoration at Bedford Park was not this elegant, of course, nor this extreme in simplicity, but it was different enough from the ordinary to attract widespread attention and cheap enough to be available to the fairly impecunious. A wag describing Bedford Park in "The Ballad of Bedford Park" in the *St. James Gazette* made this of the decoration:

> With red and blue and sagest green
> were walls and dado dyed,
> Friezes of Morris there were seen
> and oaken wainscot wide.
>
> Thus was a village builded
> for all who are aesthete
> Whose precious souls it fill did
> with utter joy complete.
>
> For floors were stained and polished
> and every hearth was tiled
> And philistines abolished
> by Culture's gracious child.[8]

There is no doubt whatever that there was a connection in people's minds between something they termed, vaguely,

Aesthetic and Bedford Park. The connection was twofold: on one hand it concerned a certain life style that included attitudes toward dress, and on the other hand it concerned architecture and decoration. This Aesthetic architecture is a significant part of any consideration of the reason for success at Bedford Park. It is important to assess just what the term *Aesthetic* implied, for *Aesthetic Movement* is one of the great misnomers in cultural history, implying as it does some sort of organized activity toward a definable goal. It was more like the bubbles in a pot of boiling water in that it was simply one form that discontent with Victorian taste assumed. It was concerned with art in the sense that these particular dissidents thought that more satisfying lives could be led if people would learn to appreciate beauty and consciously surround themselves with it. They would then be different, and their houses and clothes would naturally be different. More revaluation than movement in the short time of its greatest influence, say between 1875 and 1885, this aesthetic revaluation produced vast changes in taste roughly analogous to the changes in taste connected with the counterculture that have occurred in England and America since the early 1960s and that manifest themselves today mainly in clothing and lifestyle. The Aesthetic change affected everything from architecture to the design of clothes and furniture. With the variety of Queen Anne houses achieved at Bedford Park, the capabilities of the style were realized and the relations between Queen Anne and Aesthetic were further cemented. *Punch* was especially vitriolic about Aestheticism, and when a *Punch* cartoonist needed a locale in which to place an Aesthete he could use Bedford Park and accomplish the desired effect (see Appendix B, p. 127).

Part of the appeal of Bedford Park, of course, was the contrast between what it offered and what people wanted to get away from. The passages quoted above from *Bleak*

19

House and Wells's autobiography give the picture in general terms, but there remains to be seen an explicit escape for a future resident of Bedford Park and the American watercolorist Edwin Abbey provides it in this picture of the studio of R. A. M. Stevenson, who was later to move to Bedford Park.

> . . . One of the first men I met here in London was little Cally Bloomer, and a cheery chap in the face of disaster he was. I went one dreary, snowy, slushy, foggy day to see him that winter, at a hole of a place he lived in, with two desperate studios in the back yard—Radnor Street, Kings Road, Chelsea . . . there had just moved in that day a long-legged thin chap in a short coat, and a small black hat on the back of his head—Bob Stevenson— and he was taking out of boxes some of the most dismal sketches (of dismal snow scenery in the forest near Barbizon) I have ever seen. The studio was the most awful place you can think of, in a nasty backyard, with a dripping spout and a large puddle under it. I remember that I wanted to lean my head against the wall and cry.[9]

It is easy to imagine the reaction of anyone living in such circumstances to the advertising for Bedford Park, especially if he did not mind the accusation that he was Aesthetic or artistic. What word of mouth, gossip columns, and news items did not achieve in the way of advertisement, illustrated posters in train stations and advertisements in newspapers did (see fig. 5). One way or another word got around and people came in droves to look at Bedford Park. Many decided to stay.

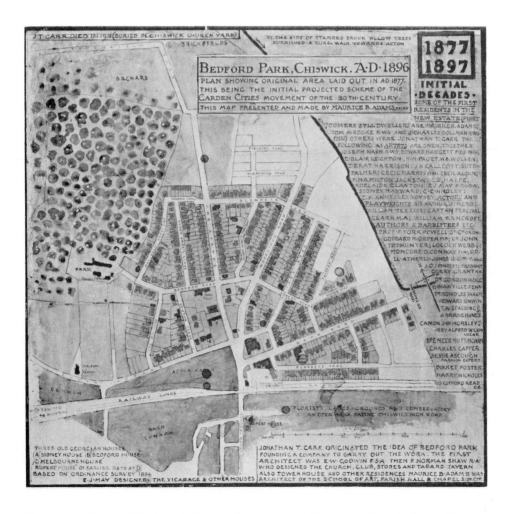

Fig. 1. Plan of Bedford Park (Courtesy of London Borough of Hounslow Library Services, Chiswick District Library)

FIG. 2.   Lithograph of Bedford Park Street Scene (Courtesy of Columbia University Libraries)

FIG. 3. Lithograph of Bedford Park (Courtesy of Columbia University Libraries)

FIG. 4. Inglenook, Moncure Conway's House in Bedford Park (Courtesy of Columbia University Libraries)

THIS Estate, the site for which was originally chosen from the well-known healthiness of the locality, possesses unusual advantages in railway accommodation, and is easy of access to town.

Situated, as it is, to the north of the Turnham Green Station, it has direct access to all the stations on the Metropolitan, Metropolitan District, London and South-Western, Chatham and Dover, and North London lines. Trains leave the station every few minutes during the day. Situated on a gravel bed, the air is always pure and dry, and free from the cold and damp inseparable from clay land.

TO OBTAIN THE MOST PERFECT SYSTEM OF DRAINAGE, Mr. Norman Shaw's system of open drainpipes has been adopted, completely separating each house from the main drain, and absolutely preventing any back draught of sewer-gas. All drain-pipes are outside the houses.

EVERY HOUSE IS BUILT ON A SOLID BED OF CONCRETE, and but few houses contain any rooms or cellars underground, adopting, on this point, one of the many advantages insisted upon by Dr. Richardson in his well-known views, so often expressed in his endeavours to secure an improvement in the construction of modern houses.

Hitherto it has been generally supposed that perfect sanitary arrangements and substantial construction are inseparable from ugliness. But it is especially claimed for Bedford Park that it is the most conspicuous effort yet made to break the dull dreariness of the ordinary suburban villa.

WITH THE VALUABLE ASSISTANCE OF MR. NORMAN SHAW, designs of houses ranging in value from £35 to £120 per annum have been supplied, in which an effort has been made to secure, by artistic treatment of plain bricks and tiles rather than by meretricious ornament, an effect hitherto never attempted.

By placing houses varying in size and design side by side the dull monotony so often seen is avoided.

In the interior of the houses it has been endeavoured to obtain a general scheme of decoration which shall render them, as they have been not inaptly described, "comfortable homes."

UNDER THE VALUABLE SUGGESTIONS OF MR. HEATON, OF BLOOMSBURY SQUARE, it has been sought to secure, by the use of matting for the lining of the walls of halls and staircases, and papers either printed especially for the estate or chosen from among the designs of Messrs. Morris, a general effect of colour and design that has hitherto only been associated with considerable expenditure; whereas it is claimed that, while everything that trouble and care can do to obtain the best possible effect is done, nothing has been attempted that would absolutely increase the cost, or cause works of solid advantage to be neglected, in order to secure decorative effect. Tiles and stained-glass windows form part of the decoration of each house.

EVERY HOUSE IS SUPPLIED WITH A BATH, FITTED FOR HOT AND COLD WATER, and the same applies to the scullery sinks.

THE CLUB, erected on the estate for ladies and gentlemen, is regarded as an acquisition by all.

THE LAWN TENNIS COURT is a very superior one, and adjoins the Club.

THE CHURCH is situated at the entrance to the Park, and the district assigned to it includes the whole estate.

The extensive Stores at the entrance to the estate afford accommodation for all furnishing and domestic purposes, and include a post and telegraph offices.

A handsome building has been erected for a SCHOOL OF ART, and proves a perfect success.

Visitors can obtain full information as to Houses and Land by applying to

Mr. B. I. MABLE, the Office, 10, Bath-road, Bedford Park,

within a few yards of Turnham Green Railway Station.

Or particulars will be given on applying to Messrs. CARR, FULTON, and CARR, Solicitors, 7, Vigo-street, Regent-street, W.

Printed for the Proprietor by THOMAS VERNON, at 19 and 20, Wine Office Court, Fleet Street, London, E.C., and published by JOHN SLATER, at the Stores, Bedford Park, Chiswick, in the County of Middlesex.

FIG. 5. Text of Advertisement for Bedford Park Appearing in Newspapers between 1875 and 1883

Fig. 6.   Corner House Designed by E. W. Godwin

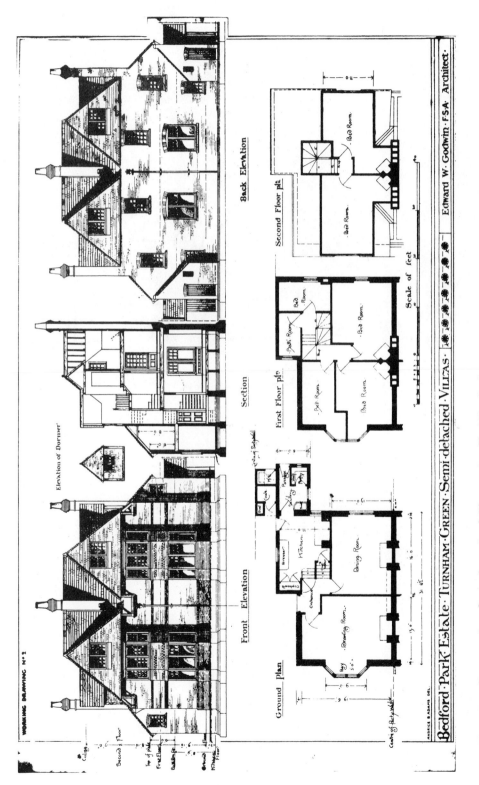

FIG. 7. Design for Semidetached House by E. W. Godwin

Fig. 8. Semidetached House Designed by E. W. Godwin

Fig. 9. Coe and Robinson Modification of Godwin's Plan for a Semi-detached House

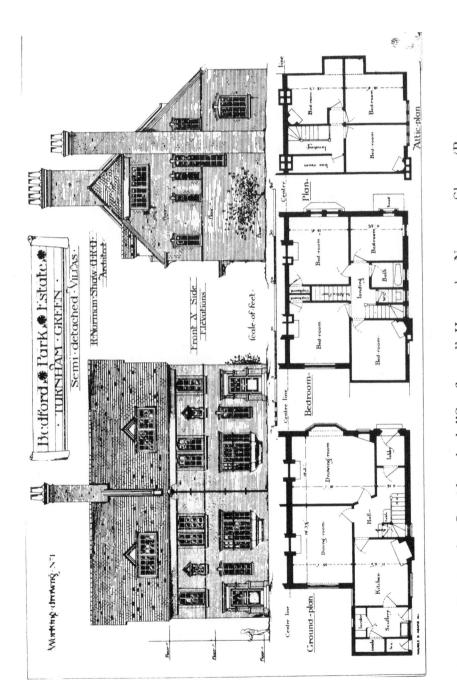

FIG. 10. Design for Semidetached "Sunflower" House by Norman Shaw (Reprinted from *Building News*)

Fig. 11. "Sunflower" House Designed by Norman Shaw

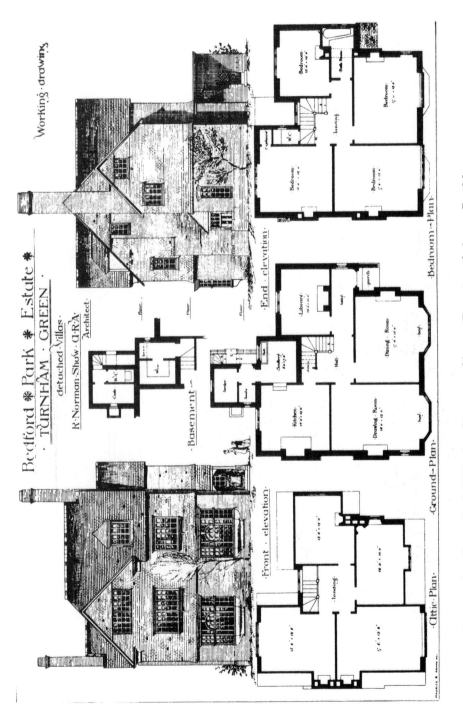

Fig. 12. Design for Detached Villa by Norman Shaw (Reprinted from *Building News*)

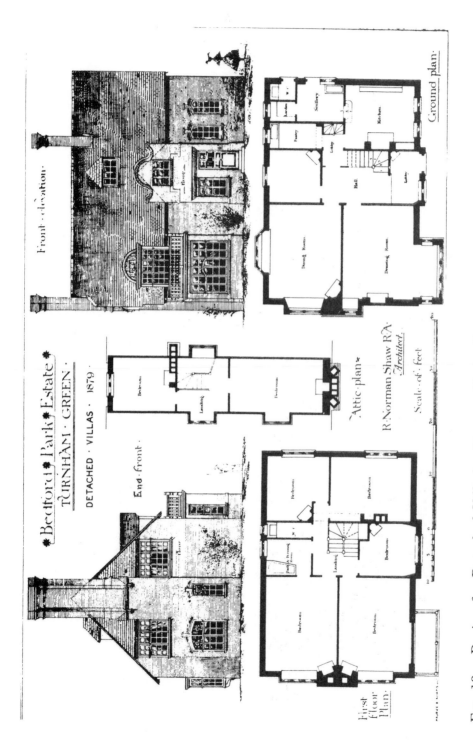

Fig. 13.   Design for Detached Villa by Norman Shaw (Reprinted from *Building News*)

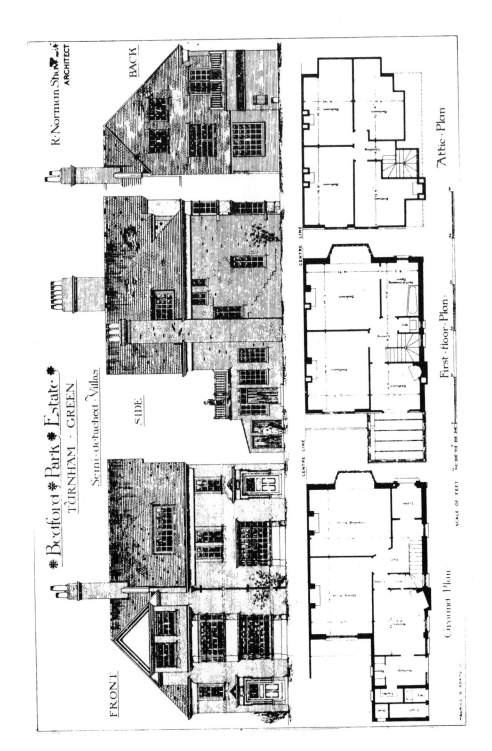

FIG. 14. Design for Semidetached Villa by Norman Shaw (Reprinted from *Building News*)

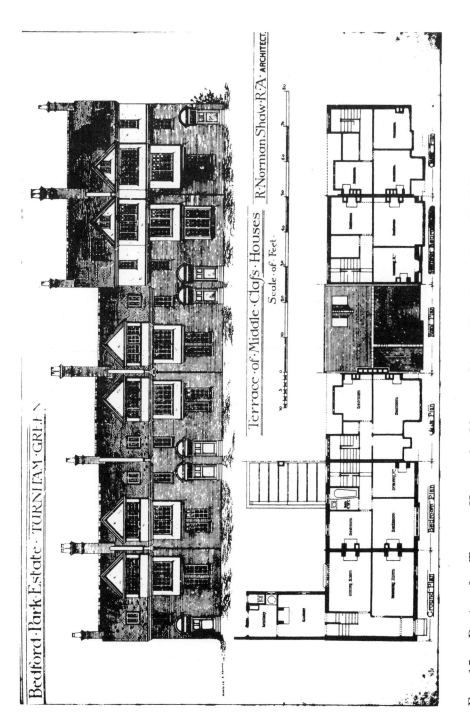

Fig. 15. Design for Terrace Houses by Norman Shaw (Reprinted from *Building News*)

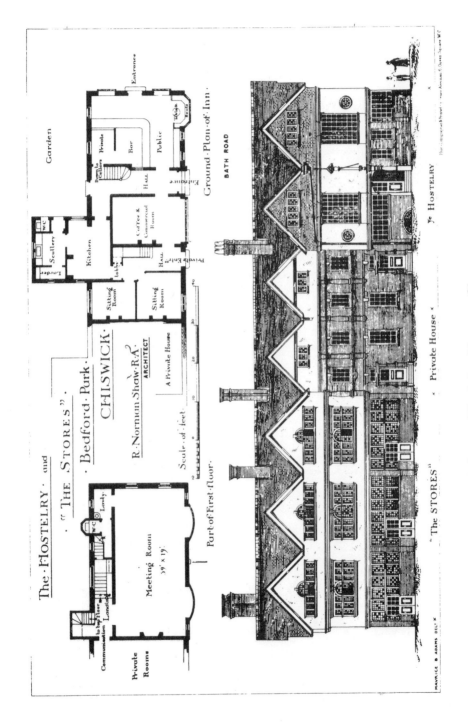

Fig. 16. Design for Tabard and Stores Block by Norman Shaw
(Reprinted from *Building News*)

FIG. 17.   Tabard and Stores Block

FIG. 18.   Details of Saint Michael and All Angels Church

F_IG_. 19.   House Designed by Norman Shaw

FIG. 20.   House Designed by Norman Shaw

FIG. 21. House Designed by Maurice B. Adams

FIG. 22. House Designed by Unknown Designer

FIG. 23.   House Designed by Unknown Designer

FIG. 24.   House Designed by C. F. A. Voysey

Fig. 25. Moncure Conway in Fancy Dress (Courtesy of
Columbia University Libraries)

Chapter 2

THE FOUNDATION AND ARCHITECTURE OF BEDFORD PARK

By 1880, Bedford Park had taken shape as an architecturally integrated, self-contained community with its own church, stores, club, tavern, and tennis courts. Built from designs of E. W. Godwin; Norman Shaw; E. J. May; Maurice B. Adams; and an architect known only by his surname, Wilson; the architecture contained an astonishing amount of variety within the basic unity of the Queen Anne Revival style. Since it was the testing ground for a number of innovations that were to become generally accepted by Western society by the middle of the twentieth century, it is tempting to see Bedford Park as the culmination of a utopian dream, a product of a master plan of social and architectural significance. Actually, its success is the more remarkable because there was no master plan behind it, for this prototype to which planners like Ebenezer Howard could turn in designing the garden city grew from the very profit motive that thinkers like William Morris and Thomas Carlyle had condemned. The real basis for the Bedford Park scheme was the "build a better mousetrap" theory of economic and social progress. In this case, the mousetrap was designed to appeal to a unique clientele, to find a way for the new, educated, but poor middle classes of the industrial age to indulge their tastes at a price they could afford. The primary answer did not lie in restructuring society, as Morris suggested, but in the imaginative use of the tools of industrialism resulting in mass production of buildings on a site that could be both rural and of easy access to the city by train. Since the middle classes lacked even the occasional relief of paternalism, they had to fend for themselves on a cash basis. Any attempt to provide them with tasteful housing which they could afford had to be a commercially feasible venture, a speculation, for there was no other way. This experiment, then, which resulted in a unique, even utopian, community, began as a speculative housing estate. Its success lay in a fortunate combination of circumstance and vision. The time had arrived for a new conception of social structure, and that concept evolved from a plan unique only in its adaptation to the needs of the new classes, particularly those members of the new classes interested in art. The predilections of the residents in turn provided the shaping force of the community. But Bedford Park developed not by radical principles built into its foundation, but by the development of principles that were latent in the mainstream of the society which Bedford Park both grew out of and escaped from.

In 1875 Jonathan Thomas Carr, a speculative builder, acquired forty-five acres of land at Turnham Green, which is a little northwest of Hammersmith. Adjoining the property was a Georgian structure called Bedford House after its original owners. The property had more recently belonged to Joseph Lindley, curator of the Royal Horticultural Society Gardens, who had planted it as gardens and orchard.[1] Jonathan Carr was one of ten children in a family noted for radical political interests and artistic inclinations. His father's household at Clapham was described by Jonathan's sister-in-law as a popular meeting place for political exiles from the continent who gathered there for the purpose of discussing the "iniquities of the existing state of European politics and planning a Utopia in which their golden dreams should come true."[2] One of Jonathan's sisters was a painter; and his brother, Joseph Comyns Carr, an art critic and editor of *The English Illustrated Magazine*, was associated with Sir Coutts Lindsay in the founding of the Grosvenor Gallery. According to his obituary in the *Chiswick Times*, Jonathan Carr was born in 1845 and was educated at Bruce Castle School, Tottenham, and King's College. He was a "cloth merchant and speculative builder," by trade, a member of the Arts Club and the Reform Club, and "An enthusiastic Radical, with many original views on social questions," who was engaged as political secretary to John Stuart Mill when Mill stood as candidate for Westminster.[3]

The first public mention of Bedford Park was a short article in *Building News* that acknowledged the novelty in this housing scheme.

A very laudable scheme has been started by Mr. John Carr, jun., of Turnham-green. The proprietor of the above estate proposes to supply for the middle classes that which the Shaftesburypark Estate has partially done for the labouring classes—namely, houses well planned, conveniently arranged, and constructed with regard to both stability and comfort and architectural character. We understand the materials are to be red Suffolk brick for the walls, and Broseley tile roofs; that each house will have a plot of ground about 50 ft. frontage, and 75 ft. deep, with gardens filled with shrubs surrounded by oak fencing and that the rents will vary from £45 to £65. About 18 houses have been already built, and these have been erected from designs by Mr. E. W. Godwin, upon three different plans. . . . It will be noticed that the plans are compact, with little waste of passage room, and architectural effect is simply obtained in an inexpensive way by the use of good materials picturesquely handled in the grouping of the features, without any affectation or ornament of which we have been sickened on most building estates. . . . The estate, which consists of 54 acres is well laid out with roads 50 ft. wide, lined with lime trees.[4]

This article, accompanied by designs for two Godwin houses, started a controversy in the correspondence column of *Building News* that lasted from 29 December 1876 until 23 November 1877 and included critical letters from architects not connected with the scheme, defenses of his housing estate by Carr (under the pseudonym The Freeholder), a disavowal of responsibility by Godwin, and the report of an investigation of the houses at Bedford Park by the Architectural Association. From this controversy it is possible to piece together a plausible picture of what Carr had in mind, and the way he set about getting it built. In 1875, or early 1876, having decided to build a new type of housing estate, he began looking for an architect to design inexpensive houses that would obviate the faults which everyone, architects and public alike, condemned in the usual suburban villa. Finding such an architect was not easy, however, as he states in this letter to the editor of *Building News*.

> But, sir, if you could have seen the face of the first architect to whom I mentioned my wants. . . . I said I wanted plans of houses that a gentleman would be glad to live in, which should be as perfect architecturally as the most splendid houses but that the extreme cost of a detached house should be £700, and for a pair of villas £1,100. Now, while I found, as I said above, every member of the profession with a sneer for "Camden Town Gothic," as the efforts of a speculative builder to be picturesque are generally called, there were few who could suggest a remedy as long as people were so inconsiderate as to want houses at such a price. Now, sir, I looked up an old file of the *Building News*, and came across Mr. Godwin's design for a country parsonage for £500, and I felt that he, at least, was able to arrange bricks and tiles in a thoroughly artistic manner, and so I secured from him designs which I maintain make The Avenue-road, Bedford Park, unrivalled round London, as containing houses conveniently and well built, in the elevation of which the only objection your correspondent can find is that small panes are used instead of large ones in some of the windows. These plans, secured at some considerable cost, I freely place in the hands of builders. . . .

I hope, sir, that I have not trespassed too long on your space. I believe I shall carry out what I have undertaken to a successful issue; and the support given by yourself and others in your kind criticism will more than enable me to bear the sneers at high art being introduced into low-priced houses.[5]

It is interesting that the only architect who was willing to undertake the task of producing "high art" at low cost was also the arch-Aesthete Godwin. Simplicity was one of the ways to cut down expense, and the external simplicity of Godwin's design can be seen in the only two of his plans which were implemented in Bedford Park (see figs. 6 through 8). As Walter Creese noted in his pioneering work on the architecture of Bedford Park, the main cause of criticism was economy.[6] Godwin was forced to cut corners in design in order to give more space to the other rooms. This made the hallways and kitchens cramped and poorly arranged. The arrangement of the kitchen in the semidetached house led one wag to write that it had an advantage, for the "servant could sit upon the table, reach things from the cupboard and from the dresser, attend to the cooking, wash up in the scullery, and look out of the window all at the same time."[7] It is clear from the correspondence that Carr bought the plans from Godwin and had them executed by a builder. This allowed Godwin to deny responsibility for what he termed "travesty" of his designs.[8] However, the criticism had been directed at the designs, and Godwin made no attempt to defend those. In addition to the meager insight which the *Building News* correspondence gives us into the foundation of Bedford Park, we also get the clear impression that in spite of criticism the project was recognized as a laudable scheme. This was stated in a letter by a noncombatant named Somers Clark, Jr., after the first criticism of Godwin's designs and Carr's defense. Mr. Clark pointed out that the critics seemed to be missing the point that Godwin's plans were *worth* crit-

icizing; that there was all the difference in the world between those plans and the ordinary builder's suburban villa,
which the profession condemned.[9]

Since the first eighteen houses were built from plans
supplied by Godwin and the firm of Coe and Robinson
(whose design was really a modification of Godwin's design
for the semi-detached house (see fig. 9), it is obvious that
the estate was not planned from the beginning, as has been
suggested, by Norman Shaw. It is impossible to determine
how deeply he was involved in planning the estate as a
whole; there is no evidence that he did any more than supply designs for buildings, as Godwin had done. It is not un-
likely that Carr himself laid out the streets and decided on
the placement of the public buildings. Shaw is not mentioned
in connection with Bedford Park until November 1877, when
Building News ran an article entitled "Bedford Park Estate,
Turnham Green," praising the scheme and noting that the
estate comprised over eighty acres, on which it was intended
to build 900 houses "supervised by Norman Shaw with local
supervision and workmanship." The article also noted the
intention "to erect a subscription reading and billiard room"
and to build a church.[10] This is the first indication that Bedford Park was being envisioned as a self-contained community rather than simply an inexpensive but attractive housing estate for the middle classes. Within two years of its
genesis, then, it was being thought of as a social unit, not
merely a dormitory suburb.

According to Moncure Conway, Carr's method of financing his scheme had a modern flavor to it. He got enough
people to agree to buy or rent houses to allow him to order
labor and materials in quantity, thus cutting costs by one
third.[11] However, this plan could not bear the heavy burden
of developing such a large estate; there were unexpected
problems, for example with drainage, which made the enter-

prise more costly than could have been predicted. So in the autumn of 1881 the Bedford Park Company, Ltd., was established with Carr as managing director; and Lord Colin Campbell, M.P.; Mr. A. H. Huth; Mr. C. B. MacLaren, M.P.; Hon. E. G. Strutt; Mr. G. W. Allen; and Mr. E. C. Grant as directors. The portion of the estate transferred to the company at that time was valued at £265,805.[12] The company was dissolved in 1886.

By July 1883, when the first issue of the *Bedford Park Gazette* appeared with a history of Bedford Park, written presumably by the editor, Fox Bourne, the estate included 113 acres, on which stood 490 houses, with a total frontage of about three miles. The first houses on The Avenue were occupied in the autumn of 1876. The first public building, the club, designed by Shaw and subsequently enlarged by E. J. May, was opened in May 1879. The church, Saint Michael and All Angels; The Tabard Inn; and the stores; all designed by Shaw, were opened in 1880, and the School of Art, designed by Maurice B. Adams, was opened in 1881.

As for the overall plan of Bedford Park, it is necessary to refute some of the myths that have appeared in descriptions of the place from early accounts in the contemporary press to recent scholarly studies. These are the notions that the streets are winding, that all of the houses are red brick, and that there are nine different types of house in the park. A glance at the map (fig. 1) shows that aside from Queen Anne's Gardens with its two jogs and a few other streets with gentle curves, the roads are quite straight. However, it must be admitted that an impression of winding streets is produced by the termination of a number of streets in **T** junctions and by the irregular block formation. As for the second myth, although the estate was probably meant to be built entirely in red brick, the fact is that some of the very earliest houses on The Avenue, even, were made of yellow brick.

Some are yellow with a pattern inlaid of red bricks to help them blend with their red neighbors. T. A. Greeves, in conversation with me in June 1967, suggested that this substitution of yellow was a practical matter. The local brickyards probably had trouble keeping up with the demand, and when the builder ran out of red bricks he simply used what he could get rather than have his workmen idle. This spirit of improvisation is evident in the truth that refutes the third myth, a claim that there are nine different house plans in Bedford Park. Actually, a rough count produces over thirty. The basis for the fallacy is probably the publication in *Building News* of three designs by Godwin (only two of which were used) and six by Norman Shaw. This not only ignores the work of other architects who designed for the estate, it contradicts the actual truth obvious to anyone who takes the trouble to look at Bedford Park. The builders, probably in conjunction with both Carr and the individual clients, made enough changes in the basic plans to constitute a veritable exercise in what can be done with the Queen Anne style. Space here does not permit close examination of all of the different examples to be found in Bedford Park, but the plans provided by Godwin and Shaw give some indication of the variety made possible by combining the elements of the Queen Anne vocabulary (figs. 6–23). Using the Queen Anne style begins to look like a game in which a player takes a certain vocabulary and puts its elements together in different combinations to make houses. The player is allowed to vary sizes and shapes of all of the elements (for example, the gables may be pointed or round, large or small), and he does not have to use all the elements in every house. The fascinating thing about the game is that it works. The neighborhood is unified by each house having been made of different combinations of the same elements, yet each house can be different in detail from its neighbors. It was even possible to integrate the larger buildings like Saint Michael and All Angels, which is late Gothic with Queen Anne details, and the Tabard, which is late Tudor with Queen Anne details. The flexibility of Queen Anne can be seen by looking closely at the first Godwin and Shaw semidetached houses on The Avenue (figs. 7 and 10). Godwin's front elevation is essentially vertical with the line of the two-story bay extended up through the attic windows. The verticality is emphasized by having the roof line of the shed-kitchen extend up the line of the front gable. The simplicity attained by the lack of ornamentation is saved from severity by the use of tile on the gable fronts and as dressing for the bays. The whole movement of the elevation is upward. Shaw's elevation, on the other hand, is strongly horizontal. This effect is achieved by the use of different fenestration for each story, by replacing the front gable with a dormer, and by declining to take the bay up through the second story. There is an impression of ornamentation in this design although the only purely ornamental device is the sunflower. Obviously, the two buildings are vastly different, yet the basic vocabulary is the same, and it was used in various combinations throughout the whole suburb. Other architects besides Godwin and Shaw who designed for Bedford Park were Maurice B. Adams; E. J. May, who probably designed most houses on the estate not directly attributable to other architects; and a man now known only as Wilson, who designed the house at 7 Queen Anne's Gardens for T. M. Rooke, the pre-Raphaelite painter.[13] According to Greeves, after the dissolution of the Bedford Park Company the remaining land was bought and developed in styles only resembling the earlier Bedford Park houses.[14] These houses, on the streets south of Bath Road and west of Marlborough Crescent, are often travesties of their models and are not to be considered vintage Bedford Park.

It is certainly Norman Shaw's touch that gives the dominant architectural flavor to the place, for in addition to the many private houses built to his designs, the most important public buildings, the church, club, inn, and stores, are his. And although they are not in the strictest sense Queen Anne, they are made to fit in by the use of Queen Anne details. The church, encrusted with white woodwork, is built in red brick and has little Dutch gables built into the side of the roof (fig. 18). The Tabard and stores block has the gables, bays, and irregular fenestration so evident everywhere in Bedford Park (figs. 16 and 17). This variety within a unified scheme was appealing at a time when most other suburbs were being built with street after street of dismal, identical houses. It is one of the factors almost always singled out in contemporary accounts like the following.

> Bedford Park consists at present of about four hundred houses intended for people enjoying incomes of from £300 to £1500 a year. This may be deduced by the facts that the rents range from £45 to £90 per annum. There is nothing novel in this. The same might be said of many desolate districts in London, grievous to look upon, almost debasing to inhabit. Brixton, for instance, is almost composed of houses rented at these rates, monotonous lines of woeful tenements, varied by cockney villas more comfortable perhaps within, but equally excruciating to the eye from their pretentiousness. The novelty of Bedford Park resides in its entire, and absolute escape from sameness or vulgarity. The houses do not look as if they had been hurriedly run-up in the gross, like Peter Pindar's razors, merely to sell. . . . The whole place has the snug warm look of having been inhabited for at least a century. This comes partly from the colour and material of the houses, a mellow red brick; partly from their architecture, which may be called "Queen Anne," abounding in gables, and permitting all kinds of inequality in height and irregularities of frontage; and partly from the intermixture of fine old trees looking almost as ancient.[15]

It is frequently noted in contemporary accounts that Carr kept as many of the trees from Lindley's orchard as he could.

This gave the place a settled look and avoided the sterility of most new developments.

But these houses which were so painstakingly designed to look old in an interesting and artistic way contained the latest developments in sanitary arrangements. The advertisement which appeared monthly in the *Bedford Park Gazette*, surmounted each month by a lithograph of Bedford Park life, gives some particulars of the unique construction of these houses (fig. 5). Building on a concrete base without a basement made a house cheaper, got the kitchen up onto the ground level, and eliminated one source of dampness. The houses were also fitted with external drainpipes (a Shaw invention, according to Blomfield) which contained traps to prevent the back-up of sewer gas into the house.[16] The spirit of experimentation, however, reached its height in the house designed for Dr. Gordon Hogg by E. J. May in 1882 to accommodate Dr. Hogg's asthmatic children. For this house had a system of central heating that could be turned into a cooling system in summer and provided a complete change of air every twenty minutes. This house was, of course, cause for attention in the architectural press, and a notice in a medical journal, *The Lancet*, pointed out the advantages of central heat about a hundred years before it would become acceptable to the English public. *The Lancet* noted the fact too, that "such reform will be opposed by the rooted habits of the country."

This kind of experimentation was one of the dimensions that made Bedford Park so important, for this use of the most advanced ideas in construction and sanitation in a community of houses that still had to be built in a revival style, even one so loosely conceived as Queen Anne, marked a turning point. The logical step after this use of a style so flexible that it could be designed from interior to exterior so long as the exterior conformed to certain loose but real principles, was the development of a style which does not have to conform, even on the exterior, to an externally imposed concept of style. That this was the next logical step can be seen from the fact that, as Greeves notes, each differently sized window which Shaw used in the sunflower semidetached plan (fig. 10) is perfectly matched to the space it illuminates.[17] Bedford Park, being experimental in every way, was the natural place for such a house, a house of no style to appear, and it was built there in 1891. This was, of course, the house designed for J. W. Forster at 12 South Parade by C. F. A. Voysey. The problems facing Voysey in the Forster house were the same ones that Godwin and Shaw had met at the beginning: beauty, convenience, space, and, especially, economy. The problem of space involved finding a place for a studio. This had been solved in some Bedford Park houses by putting it on the ground, first, or second floors, or even in a separate house in the garden. The most advantageous place was on the second floor, but one problem with the gabled houses was that frequently the second floor seemed like an attic. Voysey's solution, an elegant, white, formal, rectangular box with a low hipped roof stands out against the picturesqueness of Bedford Park like a stylistic declaration of independence (fig. 24). Yet many of the traditional elements of the Queen Anne vocabulary are translated here into elements of no style. For example, there is a bay, and the fenestration is irregular, including a thin band of windows and a round one in the Shaw manner. Actually, as Fletcher notes in "Bedford Park, Aesthete's Elysium," the front elevation is somewhat reminiscent of the Tabard. By raising the roof, Voysey was able to eliminate the attics and give his second-floor studio full height. The only ornamentation on the house is a set of thin, delicate gutter brackets. In fact, Voysey was so determined that no ornaments should be stuck onto his design by builders that he included eighteen pages of draw-

ings so that the "contractor may not put in the usual thing
—'ovulo mouldings,' 'stop chamfers,' 'fillets,' and (what without irreverence might be termed) damnation generally,"[18]
The contract price for the house was £494 10s. It is indis-
putable that the Forster house solves the old problems in a
new way. In the fifteen years between the beginning of
Bedford Park and the construction of this house it had become possible to conceive of a house without a style imposed
on it by an external conception of style, and it is significant
that this new possibility was achieved in a community of
houses which illustrated the variety of the most flexible of
traditional styles. Voysey himself had some interesting things
to say about tradition and style.

> . . . The traditionalist is shocked by what he calls a mixture
> of styles. Fitness does not appeal to the mind already welded to
> definite modes of expression. The fact the two forms of arch were
> seldom, if ever, used together in ancient times, blinds his eyes to
> the fact that altered conditions of modern life may demand the
> consideration of requirements non-existent in previous ages. The
> individualist is always ready to cast off the shackles of a previous
> time and is willing to meet the needs of the present while still
> holding fast to all enduring qualities.[19]

The Forster house was attractive in 1891 and is so today, but
there was a predictable reaction to it in Bedford Park. This
is an excerpt from a letter from York Powell to W. P. Ker:

> . . . There is a curious house here, white in Italian style, thick
> walls, studio and all complete: cost £500. It is a curiosity. When
> you come over you must see it. [Voysey] built it. The other archi-
> tects are furious, but it is original, cheap, and decidedly comely.
> When you settle in the country you must build one in a corner of
> your estate, overlooking the sea for your friends.[20]

But to return to the earlier Bedford Park, the variety of
choice in exterior design was matched by the variety in in-

terior decoration available to the residents. A certain sum
was allowed for the decoration of each room, and the client
was allowed to choose the decorations. If he wished, he
could spend more, paying the excess. Moncure Conway, the
source of this information, speculated that the taste ran so
heavily for Morris decorations that Morris would have to
build a shop near Bedford Park to handle the trade.[21] The
success of the scheme at Bedford Park is demonstrated by
the fact that in December 1881 more than 300 houses had
been erected, and although they were being built at the rate
of 150 a year, the demand still exceeded the supply.[22] However, the boom was over by 1886 when letters began to appear in the *Acton & Chiswick Gazette* complaining about the
Bedford Park estate's habit of letting the "lower element"
live rent free in vacant houses until they could be rented, to
cut down vandalism. It was observed that "these people"
who let their children run wild were obviously in a neighborhood which did not suit their style. In the reply from the
manager of the estate it is revealed that some houses were indeed vacant, and the "deserving poor" were chosen from a
long list to live in them. At a sale of lots in 1895 not one lot
was sold. However, in an interview in June 1895, Mr. Jockel,
manager of the Bedford Park Estate, assured the *Acton &
Chiswick Gazette* reporter that although there were many
lots for sale, all of the available houses for rent were taken,
and the demand far exceeded the supply. But one has the
feeling that the vintage days of Bedford Park were over. Mr.
Jockel's comments about the Queen Anne style may hold the
secret of why this was so: "The Queen Anne style has certainly come in for a lot of criticism, and it requires a certain
amount of artistic taste to appreciate the style, but then, you
know, we are all more or less artistic in the Park."[23]

But outside the "Park" practically no one was artistic,
and Mr. Jockel would have been hard put to find many peo-

ple who would have moved to Bedford Park in 1895 for one of the reasons the original residents had moved there. The Oscar Wilde trials eroded a great deal of whatever interest there was left in the Aesthetic or artistic. The wheel had turned, but although interest in Aestheticism and Queen Anne architecture had waned, the architectural unit continued to function, and to this day Bedford Park is a pleasant place in which to live.

Chapter 3

THE SHAPING FORCES OF THE COMMUNITY

The same circumstances which led to the architectural foundation and planning of Bedford Park helped make the community which grew there an immediate success. In the first place, there was the special class of people already mentioned, a new class, according to Conway, consisting of relatively poor but well educated, sensitive people who wanted something different in the way of houses and community than they were able to obtain in other suburbs and developments. They wanted not only convenient, inexpensive, artistic houses, but a community of neighbors who shared their intellectual interests; and they wanted, by these means, to escape what they considered the ugliness of the mainstream of Victorian life. In the second place there was a connection with Aestheticism and its notion that life could be made better (more pleasurable, more intense) by introducing into it beautiful things and, furthermore, that people who were sensitive enough to appreciate these beautiful things were somehow different in an admirable way from those who were not. And, while it is true that Aestheticism was the butt of so much public levity and public reaction that most people were backing away from identification with the label by 1884, it is also true that the movement had certain tendencies that were important to the early appeal of Bedford Park. When the image of Aestheticism became tarnished, Bedford

Park naturally suffered from the association—but the association had been a drawing card. The third circumstance that counted heavily in the early success of the community was a combination of the personality of Jonathan T. Carr and the important fact that since he was building a community for himself and not simply a speculative housing estate, he was able to attract as residents people who wanted much the same sort of life he wanted for himself and his own family.

The effect of Jonathan Carr's personality was felt in Bedford Park from the very beginning until long after the liquidation of his original company, The Bedford Park Estate Company, in 1886. He was always very much "there" where matters of the community were concerned and was a neverending source of ideas for projects which might interest the residents. He worked closely with the Vigilance Committee that was formed to protect the public interests of residents in matters of finance, rates, drainage, and so forth; and he was behind the foundation of the other general committee, the Bedford Park Committee, which was formed in 1883 to discuss all other matters relating to Bedford Park. It was this committee which devised community projects and formed smaller committees for working out ways of getting things done. Carr was the publisher of *The Bedford Park Gazette*, and little is known about the early organization of the Bedford Park Club except that he was the proprietor and had the final say over activities there. Application had to be made to him for use of the rooms in the club for lectures, meetings, and parties. It would be hard to draw a line between the public life of Bedford Park and Carr's private life. For example, when the annual Fancy Dress Ball was held at the club the decorations and, indeed, the party extended out onto the lawn of Tower House, his residence. His lawn was the site of the annual garden show; he could always be counted on to make a speech and award the prizes, and one suspects that his generosity may have led to his financial downfall. As an illustration of this generosity, he played host to 170 children at a Children's Jubilee Treat on 26 June 1887: "The repast over, some very clever feats of *legerdemain* highly amused the juveniles, as well as other attractions. On leaving, the children were each presented with mugs commemorative of the Jubilee, and a new sixpence."[1]

The connections between Bedford Park and Aestheticism were certainly more than myth, but *Aesthetic* must not be taken to mean *decadent*. Indeed, its use in relation to Bedford Park may lead to better understanding of what the term *Aesthetic* meant in the last quarter of the nineteenth century.

Bedford Park was known as an Aesthetic paradise almost before the mortar was dry in the first house, if as it seems to be, the following quotation from *Punch* is a caricature of Bedford Park. If it is not, then it is equally interesting as a model into which the public mind would fit Carr's housing estate. The article which ran serially in three installments is called "The Rise and Fall of the Jack Spratts, A Tale of Modern Art and Fashion." This is a description of Jack and his home.

> In a beautiful suburb of London, undesecrated, as yet by steam or telegraph-wires, and surrounded by low-lying flowery meads, through which the Thames would still meander occasionally, as it had been wont to do in days gone by, dwelt Jack Spratt, a handsome, genial, and simple-minded young painter. . . . Their house was of red brick, smothered in ivy, and had been built about Queen Anne's time, or before, and never repaired since, nor meddled with in any way whatever. It stood by itself in a small old-fashioned garden, surrounded by once peach-laden walls that crumbled to the touch, and overrun nettles, thistles, marigolds, sunflowers, and poppies; a trellised arbour of sweet peas half buried a sun-dial in its fragrant gloom; and there was a nice little green pond. Apple-trees and pear-trees, leafless and long past fruit-bearing, but beautifully gnarled, grew rank as in an orchard, and on to a luxuriant lawn that had never known the scythe,

opened the pretty studio, which was full of blue china, round mirrors, faded tapestry, arms and armour, an organ with beautifully painted pipes but no bellows, and other musical instruments, such as sackbuts and psalteries. . . . The dust lay thick on these pretty things, and toned them into harmony. Studio, house, and garden were pervaded with a subtle fragrance, significant of old associations, which arose in the soft summer twilight from time-honoured, ruined, and all but forgotten drains.[2]

Except for the factor of age, this description of house, orchard, and even poor drainage applied to Bedford Park; Spratt could well be a caricature of the young, impecunious painters who flocked to Bedford Park and decorated their houses in the artistic style. In 1882, Walter Hamilton described Bedford Park as "The Home of the Aesthetes" in his book *The Aesthetic Movement in England.* Hamilton's treatment was sympathetic; others were not. Bedford Park and Aestheticism were frequently ridiculed, and in the first issue of *The Bedford Park Gazette* (July 1883) the editor took pains to deny that Bedford Park was, or ever had been, Aesthetic. However, some attitudes and behavior of the residents in the early days lead one to suspect that there was more to the accusations than the residents later cared to admit. Evidence for this lies in a lecture given by Jonathan Carr at the club on 27 January 1883. This lecture, "The Harm Aestheticism Has Done to the Spread of Art," far from ridiculing it, makes a careful distinction between true Aestheticism, or the seeking of beauty, and the silliness (epitomized by Oscar Wilde) which characterized the outward show of a sort of false Aestheticism.

. . . The speaker then proceeded to describe that many persons consider the meaning of the word to be the wearing of a drab coat, light hat, tie, etc., whereas it was the profession of art of the highest character that was the true meaning of the word aestheticism. It was owing to the former idea, and not to the

63

latter reality, that harm accrued to the spread of art (hear, hear). Some men possessed the talents and abilities so as to be able to lift the veil, as it were, and tell us of a world beyond and this was enchanting, and when the world was looked at in a correct light by educated minds, it made them desire to take part in it. . . . It was not the blue and white china, or the peacock's feathers, that constituted the word aestheticism, nor the men who sought after prettiness. Many were of the opinion that by gaining a little they had reached the top of the ladder, whereas they had really only ascended one round of it. He submitted that the struggle was great, but the pleasure after the victory was greater (hear, hear). . . . The speaker then spoke in high terms of the work and productions of Rossetti, Burne-Jones and others as being examples in support of the cause of aestheticism, and concluded by urging those who had attained a little prettiness around them in the uphill walk of life not to stop and rest, but to persevere for something better, and something nobler.[3]

The last sentence is apt advice from the founder of an Aesthetic community to his little flock.

In the same year we find another influential resident of Bedford Park, Moncure Conway, preaching a sermon, "The Gospel of Art," to his congregation at South Place Chapel; this sermon is so Aesthetic in nature that it might conceivably have been written by Walter Pater. It begins, "The ministry of Art is the highest because, when true, it awakens in man the emotions which lift him to the highest possibilities of his existence." Conway goes on to agree with Schopenhauer that one exception to the general misery of the world is the emotion excited by a work of art. "Very few have either the culture or the opportunity for dwelling amid works of art. This may be true for the present, but it does not prevent our hope and endeavour for a coming time when art shall be brought near to the life of all men, in its highest forms."[4] This last was attempted at Bedford Park.

The persistent rumors in the contemporary press of behavior at Bedford Park that smacked of a bygone age—in fact, of Aestheticism carried to the extreme of eccentric dress and behavior—are borne out by more than theories about art and the fact that the residents lived in Queen Anne Revival houses. A prime example of the kind of thing that earned the community its Aesthetic reputation was the nature of the services in Saint Michael and All Angels, which was consecrated on 17 April 1880 in a whirl of controversy. On the Saturday that the consecration services were to be held, a letter addressed to the Bishop of London appeared in the Acton paper accusing the Reverend Alfred Wilson, minister of Saint Michael and All Angels, of "Popish and Pagan mummeries." It included an itemized list of his trangressions such as marching in procession round the church, prostrating himself before the consecrated elements, making the sign of the cross when giving the elements to the people, wearing a colored stole, and singing the Agnus Dei. The letter stated that the author had complained before to the bishop and had received no satisfaction; now he asked that the bishop refuse to consecrate the new church "until you have obtained from Mr. Wilson a pledge that he will conduct the services of the church in accord with the laws of the Church of England." It was signed by Henry Smith, Churchwarden, of Chiswick.[5] The controversy started by this letter raged in the *Acton, Chiswick & Turnham Green Gazette* for several months, and led among other things to the paper's sending a spy to Saint Michael and All Angels to see what was going on. The spy duly reported, on 12 July, that not only was the service in the church very "high," and the atmosphere reminiscent of a Roman Catholic Church to the point of confusion, but the congregation was divided into three sections, one for men, one for women, and one where they could sit together with children. On 26 June there had been printed another long letter affirming this arrangement and further reporting that the choristers bowed in lowly adoration to the altar as they went to take their places in the choir, and that the ladies in the congregation crossed themselves to the altar and were continually bowing and curtseying to each other! The accusation of popery may be explained as part of the controversy about low and high services in the Church of England. The division of the congregation according to sex and the ladies' habit of curtseying are a different matter. In one letter Henry Smith said he thought it was customary in the Roman Church to so divide the congregation. Actually, a better answer where Bedford Park is concerned may involve the "purity" associated with Aestheticism in sexual matters (one recalls the caricature in *Patience* of the vegetable love exhibited by an Aesthetic young man for a "too too French, French Bean"). The women's behavior is strange indeed for 1880, except in an idyll or realm of fantasy where people were willing to playact a bit to escape the ugliness and boredom of Victorian life, in other words in an Aesthetic community. William Butler Yeats remembered this idyllic quality about Bedford Park when he moved there with his father's household for the first of two periods of residency in 1876.

> For years Bedford Park was a romantic experiment. At North End my father had announced at Breakfast that our glass chandelier was absurd and to be taken down, and a little later described the village Norman Shaw was building. I had thought he said, "There is to be a wall round and no newspapers to be allowed in." And when I told him how put out I was at finding neither wall nor gate, he explained that he had merely described what ought to be. . . . We went to live in a house like those we had seen in pictures and even met people dressed like people in story-books. . . . We could imagine people living happy lives as we thought people did long ago when the poor were picturesque and the master of a house could tell of strange adventures over the sea.[6]

This idyllic approach to life was undoubtedly one of the pleasant aspects of Bedford Park, but another side of the picture linked it to Aestheticism also. This was the presence of a number of professional artists as well as an art school, The Chiswick School of Art, which was literally built into the community. Art mattered in Bedford Park, and this fact alone could have been one of the shaping forces in the community, for it gave many of the residents a common interest and added immensely to the cultural life of the neighborhood. Bedford Park was famous for the richness of life it offered, especially in contrast to the modest means of its residents. As Oliver Elton put it, "This pocket settlement . . . soon became the resort of painters, players, poets, journalists, schoolmasters, exiles, Bohemians mostly, . . . stray city men and bourgeois. It was known to some as the 'pauper's paradise,' but it was long rich in talk and gifts of the spirit."[7]

The Bedford Park Gazette made much of the fact that major generals as well as artists lived happily in Bedford Park, and at every opportunity quashed any suggestion that there was anything exclusive about the place. Analysis of the directory published in the *Gazette* in January 1884 shows that in a list of some 400 names there are at least those of twenty-two artists and designers, eight authors and journalists, six architects, three musicians, and two actors. Set beside these people more or less connected with the arts, there are twenty-two lawyers, thirteen military men (mostly retired), six ministers, four civil engineers, five medical doctors, a merchant, and a stockbroker. Although it is admittedly inaccurate, this list at least gives some indication of the occupations followed by the residents of Bedford Park, and it inevitably brings up the question of why Bedford Park was acclaimed far and wide as an artists' colony when it had as many lawyers, for example, as artists. Perhaps the most obvious reason lies in the fact that artists are more visible in a community than lawyers; their fame outside a community reflects on the place where they live, especially if it is noised about that many of them live and work there. Very few communities the size of Bedford Park could boast equal representation in art shows if the period from January until July 1883 is indicative. During this time, according to the *Gazette*, the residents T. M. Rooke, E. Blair Leighton, and Alfred W. Strutt had pictures in the Royal Academy Exhibition; the architect E. J. May had pictures in the Royal Academy collection of architectural drawings; and T. M. Rooke, H. M. Paget, Mrs. H. M. Paget, and F. Hamilton Jackson exhibited at the Grosvenor Gallery. Edward Hargitt, Joseph Nash, and F. Hamilton Jackson were represented in the exhibits of the Institute of Painters in Water-colours. The Society of British Artists exhibited work by E. Blair Leighton and Miss H. S. Fenn. Miss Fenn also had a picture in the York exhibition.[8]

The community's interest in art showed itself at home in a number of ways. One-man shows were frequent in Bedford Park, and it was the usual practice to hold a show in the club for works on their way to exhibitions. It is interesting that one of the first societies organized was the Sketching Club in November 1880. Each member of the Sketching Club was expected to submit at least six sketches a year on selected subjects. The drawings were exhibited for three-day periods throughout the year in the Bedford Park Club. They were hung without the artist's name but with a number, and each member was to vote for what he considered the best drawing in each exhibition by signing his initials beside the drawing's number in a book provided for that purpose. The member who obtained the greatest number of first places during the twelve-month period would win a prize.[9] The Sketching Club expired when the center of artistic interest shifted to the art school, but it illustrates the lively interest in art within the community.

The Chiswick School of Art was an integral part of the community; according to the *Gazette* it was projected in 1880, the building was finished by August 1881, and the school opened on 3 October 1881.[10] The school was operated in connection with the Science and Art Department of the Committee of The Council on Education, South Kensington. The first directors of the school were E. S. Burchett and F. Hamilton Jackson; eleven of the sixteen members of the original Committee for the Chiswick School of Art were residents of Bedford Park. The art school was included in the *Gazette's* monthly advertisement for Bedford Park, along with the club, tennis court, stores, and church, "a handsome building has been erected for a SCHOOL OF ART, and proves a perfect success."[11] The school was a matter of great interest in the community, and the *Gazette* carefully reported details of activities there. For example, H. R. H. Princess Louise visited the school on 22 May 1884 then drove round the estate and had tea with Mr. and Mrs. Carr. The lecture room of the art school was available for public use and was used for a university extension course in 1884. On at least one occasion, 8 June 1884, the annual Fancy Dress Ball was held at the school instead of the club, with the benefits going to the school's prize fund.

The prospectus of the school, printed monthly in the *Gazette*, offered the following:

Freehand Drawing in all its branches, Practical Geometry and perspective; Architectural and Mechanical Drawing; Painting in Oil, Tempera and Water-colours of Ornament, Flowers, Objects of Still Life, etc.; Pottery and Tile Painting; the Figure from the Antique and the Life; Anatomy as applicable to Art; Designing for Decorative Purposes—as in Wall-papers, Furniture, Metalwork, Stained Glass, etc.; Study of Historic Styles of Decoration.

69

This course to be extended as opportunity may offer or occasion require.[12]

Walter Hamilton on his visit to "the home of the aesthetes" was especially interested in the art school which he saw as a tool for disseminating the tenets of the new aestheticism.

> . . . In one room when I entered, the pupils were drawing from models; in another they were painting, and one young lady was just putting the finishing touches to a very life-like representation of that aesthetic favorite, that bright emblem of constancy —the brilliant sunflower.
>
> I noticed too that in many instances the young ladies were decidedly of the aesthetic type, both as to the mode of dress, and fashion of arranging their hair.[13]

There had been a plan, originally, to organize a music school in conjunction with the art school, and a music master, C. J. Hargitt, was employed. However, this never got past the stage of offering piano lessons, and the scheme was soon abandoned. The school of art passed through many stages of development and adaptation but remained a part of the community for many years. In 1891 it became the Chiswick School of Arts and Crafts, primarily a school of applied arts featuring leather work, embroidery, bookbinding, and metalwork. Costumes were made there for Ellen Terry's and Henry Irving's theatrical performances, as well as items like maces and chains for city corporations.[14] In 1895 the school became the Chiswick Polytechnic and is still in session.

The presence of a number of artists in the community of Bedford Park made itself felt in other ways. It made a difference in the fabric of the community that men were working there during the day; that it was not a dormitory suburb is probably one of the reasons that the strong sense of community developed so easily. Bedford Park provided an atmosphere conducive to work, or at least to the appearance of work, as the following letter from York Powell to Oliver Elton illustrates.

> We are all jolly here together. Yeats is well, Orpen has his Irish book done, Paget pegging away at theatre 'blocks' for *Graphic*, Todhunter pegging away at fitting Schiller's *Mary Stuart* for the modern stage, by unmelodramming it and poetizing it. ——— engaged all day, and nipping about like a lamplighter, and going up to London to the theatre late of an evening to shake off the influence.[15]

All the men mentioned in this letter were residents of Bedford Park in the early years before 1885. The Yeats mentioned here is John Butler Yeats the painter and father of William Butler Yeats; Orpen is G. H. Orpen the lawyer and Celtic scholar; H. M. Paget was a well-known set designer and black and white illustrator; Dr. John Todhunter was a playwright and poet. One wonders who ——— was.

York Powell himself is an interesting example of the kind of man who found Bedford Park congenial. Powell (1850–1904), lecturer in law at Christ Church from 1874 to 1894, then Regius Professor of History from 1894 until his death, was co-editor, with Gudbrandr Vigfusson, of Icelandic texts and author and translator in his own right. A self-avowed "socialist and jingo," he was a friend of Verlaine and Rodin and collected Japanese prints.[16] But although the center of his professional life was Oxford, he chose to live in Bedford Park from January 1881 until some time in 1902, spending the middle of the week in Oxford and returning to Bedford Park for long weekends. It is probable that the wide range of York Powell's interests made the society of Bedford Park more congenial to him than that of Oxford. This fragment of a letter from him to Gudbrandr Vigfusson illustrates a part of what it was he found there: "There is a nice fellow here, an Irishman, with whom I can talk. It is like being in a foreign country, when you have to bottle up all your thoughts for months because there is no one who understands the tongue of literary men or matters."[17] It is interesting that the place where he could find no one who understood literary matters was Oxford! The Irishman could have been any one of a number of Powell's neighbors; the significant point is that he found this congeniality in Bedford Park and he found it not only in the personalities of his neighbors but in the type of life that they led. He liked the healthy and natural atmosphere evidenced, he thought, by the number of children in it, and he found satisfaction in the day-to-day life, as this vignette in a letter to W. P. Ker illustrates. It was written shortly after the deaths of Gudbrandr Vigfusson and Powell's own wife.

> I will give you a photograph of his [Vigfusson's] picture, which Paget did for me: a fine oil sketch as he sat working with me two afternoons in Bedford Park, he speaking, I writing, Paget painting swiftly and hard all the while with the painter's inspiration on him, and Paget's wife working children's clothes and talking now and then, and the children running in and out of the room; one of the brightest days since my dear wife went from me.[18]

Life and work appear to have been beautifully woven together in this scene.

The presence of artists in the community was evident in the casual dress for which Bedford Park was noted. When the *Gazette* tried to throw off the stigma of *Aesthetic* as a descriptive term for Bedford Park, it chose *Bohemian* to replace it. The artists' touch was also noticeable in the costumes at the Fancy Dress Balls and in the sets and costumes they designed for the Amateur Dramatic Club. On 10 and 11 January 1882, the artists provided an evening of *tableaux vivants* in the large room at the club. *Tableaux vivants* were a favorite entertainment of the time and were produced in the following manner: a curtain of gauze was stretched between the performers and the audience to give a muted, ethereal appearance to everything performed on the stage. A reader standing in front of the gauze curtain read from a selected work, and the performers behind the curtain posed in attitudes illustrating the text. This is the program for those January evenings:

"Kate Bar-lass" (arranged by Mr. Manfred Trautschold and Mr. T. Erat Harrison); "The Little Man and the Little Maid" (Mr. F. Hamilton Jackson; "1. Banishment. 2. Reconciliation" (Mr. E. Blair Leighton); "Queen Guinevere and Child Rowland" (Mr. H. M. Paget); "The Warlock's Mirror" (Mr. James Nash and Mr. J. C. Dollman); and "Child Rowland to the Dark Tower Came" (Mr. F. Hamilton Jackson and Mr. Moncure D. Conway).[19]

It is essential, however, to remember that many people lived for years in Bedford Park without taking any active part in community life. But although people like Arthur Pinero and William Terriss lived very quiet private lives in Bedford Park, their presence may have served to enhance the reputation of the community. Other residents not only did not take part in the community but resented some of those who did; not everyone came to Bedford Park looking for either Bohemia or a "pauper's" paradise, as the following comment from the Outsider's column in the *Bedford Park Gazette* indicates.

Another correspondent has a less intelligible grievance, or, at any rate, one less likely to excite sympathy. "The original idea of Bedford Park," he says, "was a retreat, to a certain extent, from 'the madding crowd's ignoble strife,' where men of a superior social position, distinctly recognized, should, with their families, be enabled to enjoy 'home life' after the quiet old English fashion, and yet be within easy reach of the amusements of the metrop-

73

olis. With this object in view, houses have been built to suit small as well as large families, so that each householder may be a distinct unit—the key to the whole plan. But, if two or three distinct families club together, and, emigrating from those localities sacred to the 'compound lodger class,' take a house in Bedford Park, and then apportion it among themselves, room by room, the unity of the social design is at once destroyed, and, instead of English homes—and English because separate and exclusive, in a good sense—the locality would, in the course of a very short time, become like Battersea, Dalston, and such compound lodger places, where people without any defined social status, and altogether below the lowest grade in the authoritative table of precedence, would, with multiplied perambulators and rivalry in dress travestie things beyond them, and grate the ear with the sham shibboleth so very different from the tone of the real. This is to be guarded against."[20]

The Outsider's answer was that if the correspondent is correct in thinking that the ideal had been that "Bedford Park was meant to be an aggregation of units, holding aloof from one another on account of their 'superior social position,' or anything of that sort, it strikes me that the project has failed completely, and that its failure is a matter of hearty congratulation." He goes on to cite the congeniality in both club and private home which ignores wealth, or lack of it, and style of dress. His view, probably valid, was that the "ideal" of Bedford Park had been Bohemian and that this ideal was being achieved as artificial social barriers had been broken down—yet individuality had still been maintained.[21]

The residents in Bedford Park, artists or not, achieved a community, in the real sense of the word, where the quality of life transcended any superficial connection with Aestheticism, art, or anything else; yet it could not have been achieved without interests in common to a large number of the residents, and it is an inescapable conclusion that the connections, whatever their true nature, with Aestheticism were, at least initially, good advertisement.

The community which Jonathan Carr and his friends achieved at Bedford Park was unique in its time and would be unusual in any age, but the vision of the "good life" which they shared has now become so commonplace it is startling to realize that in its early days Bedford Park was an experiment as different from contemporary society as the present-day commune is from established forms of communities. In its simplest terms Bedford Park was a middle-class, suburban community of people who retained their individuality while sharing some common interests as well as recreational facilities and social services.

Chapter 4

COMMUNITY LIFE: THE PURSUIT OF "CORPORATE HAPPINESS"

Perhaps the most startling term for the early achievement at Bedford Park was used by the Outsider to describe its distinctive quality of life as "corporate happiness." In attributing this achievement to the amount of freedom allowed the individual and to the astonishing amount of neighborly feeling, he remarks that in every other community he knows, both inside and outside of London, "everybody rushes as far away as he can from his own street and suburb to seek his amusements and form his friendships." The aim in Bedford Park, however, is to find these things at home. The only danger he can see to the situation lies in the inhabitants' tendency to spend too much time together.[1] This prediction proved valid by the summer of 1884 when the community was split by disagreement over the curriculum of a new school, but the period between the formation of the Bedford Park Club in 1879 and the last issue of the *Gazette* in July 1884, saw the foundation of the community and the establishment of organizations which lasted long after the first ideals had faded.

While the initial impetus to move to Bedford Park may well have been simply the search for an attractive, inexpensive place to live, it was not long before the estate offered a great deal more. Although there is no evidence that Jonathan Carr began with utopia in mind, the fact remains that Bedford Park did become, for a while, a kind of middle-class utopia. Where most suburbs are culturally and emotionally arid, Bedford Park was rich; it was not only to escape the city that people moved here, it was to find something they thought it offered. That thing, the quality they found, was a *community* in the real sense of the word. Ian Fletcher has noted the remarkable extent to which the residents felt themselves members of a community: "Bedford Park provoked images. . . . It was seen as Arcadian, Aesthetic, Bohemian; as an unconscious example of a Romantic Socialist Co-operative."[2] It is this last image, not totally accurate, as Fletcher also notes, that interests us here. It is illustrated by Moncure Conway's theory that the system of cooperation in Bedford Park marked a degree of social evolution toward St. Simonian socialism.

> The new suburb which has thus come into existence swiftly . . . has gone far toward the realization of some aims not its own, ideals that have hitherto failed. There is not a member of it who would not be startled, if not scandalized, at any suggestion that he or she belonged to a community largely socialistic. They would allege, with perfect truth, that they are not even acquainted with the majority of their neighbors, have their own circle of friends, and go on with their business as men and women of the world. Nevertheless, it is as certainly true that a degree in social evolution is represented by Bedford Park, and that it is in the direction of that co-operative life which animated the dreams of Père Enfantin and St. Simon. All society, indeed, must steadily and normally advance in that direction. . . . We have also our co-operative stores; our newspapers and current literature are obtained in common; and perhaps by the time this paper is read the Tabard may be supplying the *table d'hôte* at a rate sufficiently moderate to place a daily dinner within reach of families who may find that desirable. Thus the co-operative principle has shown its applicability to the requirements of the cultured class.[3]

This statement is doubly interesting because it describes the cooperation at work in Bedford Park and illustrates

Conway's feeling that he, as a member of this community, is taking part in an experiment which marks a significant point in social history. This was a peculiarly "modern" quest for cooperation and communion rather than isolation and competition in living arrangements. The attempt to form a community in which the individual gives his time, talents, energy, and even money to form a society which in turn responds to his needs by giving him something to enjoy and identify with is reaching a further extension now, almost a hundred years later, in the communes. The resident of Bedford Park was not required to pay the price of his individuality, as members of communes are; he could remain master of his own castle as well as a member of the community, but he was aware that he was building a new kind of society, and the more idealistic, like Moncure Conway and Fox Bourne, felt that it was the way of the future and that Bedford Park would be followed in this by other experiments. The society they were trying to build was outside the mainstream of English life and the words *colony* and *village* as well as *utopia* keep cropping up to describe their community, as in this editorial in the *Gazette*.

> Bedford Park claims to be a unique suburb of London—small, but with all the nearer approach to completeness because of its smallness. It is a tiny colony, in which the colonists, by a happy union of design and accident, belong to widely different walks in life, and are as diverse in their sympathies as in their vocations. . . . The individuality that is asserted and developed more freely than it might have been had the individuals continued in their old haunts and routes, we believe occasions greater cohesion than could be looked for were there less independence. . . . No one can say that there is not energy enough in Bedford Park, working fitfully at times, but on the whole yielding welcome results, and full of promise. If we claim to be thus a colony of a new and hopeful sort, we also aspire to a sort of modern revival of the very ancient conception of a village community. . . . We

78

are neither a despotism, nor an oligarchy, nor a plutocracy, and the basis of our institutions is altogether democratic. They spring up, and they thrive or wither; but they thrive or wither according as they meet with much or little approval, and satisfy or fail to satisfy the requirements of the community in general.[4]

There was no formal government in Bedford Park, but there were two committees to look after the welfare of the residents vis-à-vis the local authorities of Chiswick and Acton and to aid in making that part of the social life that was public run smoothly. The first of these, the Vigilance Committee, was formed in June 1881 "for the purpose of cooperating with Mr. Carr in all matters affecting the public interest and general welfare of the residents."[5] The main problem confronting this committee was drainage for the estate. The other general committee, formed in April 1883, was the Bedford Park Committee, composed of ninety residents, with Carr as chairman. This committee was empowered to discuss all matters relating to Bedford Park with the exception of financial and sanitary matters, which were to be left to the Vigilance Committee. It was originally supposed to discuss proposals for new activities, and when a proposal was considered feasible, a smaller committee was to be formed to investigate the practical means of carrying it out. This was the origin of the *Gazette*, the Natural History Gardening Society, the conversational lectures on literature and art, and the reorganized Musical Society. In actual fact the Bedford Park Committee shortly became a forum for discussing anything and everything that had to do with Bedford Park, and although it had no power for anything except discussion, this was enough to lead to dissension, for people in the pursuit of "corporate happiness" tended to fall into the assumption that they had more in common with all their neighbors in Bedford Park than was really the case. The

danger of submitting what might, on the face of it, seem to
be a fairly private scheme to this arbiter of the public good
is illustrated by the long, hot battle fought over a proposed
school. This controversy is worth going into because it illustrates some of the basic aims of the more progressive members
of the community and the problems they had to face.

The October *Gazette* reported a meeting at the club on 20
September 1883 of people interested in forming a limited
liability company to set up a school for boys and girls in
Bedford Park. At this meeting a prospectus was read, discussed, and altered. This prospectus contained three innovations in the education of the young: boys and girls would
attend classes together; there would be no religious instruction whatever, although facilities would be made available
for parents who wished to have their children instructed in
religion outside school hours; and children would attend
class only from 9:30 to 12:30 daily. They could return to
school from 3:00 until 4:30 to do their homework under the
teacher's supervision if the individual parents chose to send
them. Those who did not return in the afternoon were to re-
ceive no help at home with their work, were not to spend
more than an hour and a half at it, and would be forbidden
to do it in the evenings. This last innovation of shorter hours
in class than usual was designed to accommodate the special
circumstance that Bedford Park children could be expected
to glean from their richer home life what many children had
to expect from school. Integrated classrooms of boys and
girls were to follow the pattern already proved in Scotland
and America. The plan was discussed everywhere, and the
Gazette came out strongly in favor of it; after all, the editor's wife was a member of the board of directors. The local
messianic impulse can be seen in the *Gazette's* hope that
the school might one day "serve as a model for similar
enterprises in other parts of England."[6]

A limited liability company was formed and the articles
of incorporation and prospectus duly appeared in the February *Gazette*. Then the trouble started. The bone of conten-
tion was the refusal to give theological instruction at all or
even to begin the day with a prayer. This course of action
had been chosen, not, as one of the board members, Dr. Gordon Hogg, pointed out in a letter to the editor, because the
directors were opposed to religion, but because belief took
so many different forms in Bedford Park that "any attempt
to frame a scheme of religious teaching sufficiently colour-
less not to offend anybody would result—assuming such a
scheme possible—in satisfying no one."[7] In the course of a
public row over this at a meeting of the Bedford Park Committee, it was decided to form another limited liability company and open a school on more conventional lines. The
first school, the innovative one, called The Bedford Park
School, opened on 22 April 1884, and the board remained ada-
mant: there was no religious instruction. The other one,
called The Bedford Park High School, opened in July 1884.
Its prospectus, which appeared in the *Gazette*, provided for
a school on a Christian basis "with a conscience clause,"
where boys and girls, though taught the same subjects, would
not attend class together above the level of kindergarten.
Its only innovation was a shorter school day.[8]

The *Gazette* rather weakly pointed to the benefits to be
derived from having two schools in competition for excel-
lence rather than just one, but the ferocity of the attack
on the principles of the Bedford Park School and indeed on
the characters of the people who proposed it (they were
publicly accused of being "godless") was a surprise to Fox
Bourne and probably to a number of others also. The two
schools symbolize, in a way, the basic differences in the community; one was the kind of school an experimental community might devise to fit its peculiar needs; the other was

81

conventional, aimed at perpetuating the very kind of society some thought they were trying to escape or alter. Bedford Park was obviously not a monolithic community; the "corporate happiness" was in jeopardy at this early date.

It was the opinion of the Outsider that the school committee had got itself into this mess by bringing the matter to the Bedford Park Committee. They had done it merely to let the community know what they intended to do (they were, after all, a private group). But telling the committee about it seemed to give that body authority in the matter which it simply did not possess. He aptly notes that nowhere else in London would such a group have been so foolish as to assume that their neighbors would agree with them on a topic like this.

The two schools coexisted until July 1895, when they merged to become first the United Schools and then the Chiswick and Bedford Park High School. It is significant that in 1895 many of the original combatants were again present at a meeting to discuss the merger and agreed that Bedford Park had enough money and pupils for one good school, but not for two.[9] Cooperation in the matter of the school did not work, but there were too many cohesive forces in the community for this upheaval, even with all its repercussions, to cause a permanent rift. One repercussion was a shuffling of members on the board of the Chiswick School of Art because they had been drawn into the fight over the elementary school. The board disagreed over whether they could legally lease rooms to the Bedford Park School for classes, and the resulting disagreement led to the resignation of the chairman and secretary of the board of the art school. But other men took their places; the community adapted and absorbed the differing opinions.

The most outstanding example of cooperation in Bedford Park was the Bedford Park Club, organized in 1879.

This club was the center of social life and, as Conway called it, the "heart" of the community. For an entrance fee of three guineas and an annual subscription of two guineas (half a guinea for ladies), the members had use of a clubhouse from 9:00 A.M. until midnight which provided light refreshments; games such as billiards, piquet, and whist; a library containing the principal daily and weekly papers, monthly and quarterly magazines, and a series of new books provided by the Grosvenor Gallery Library (later by Mudie's). There was even a billiard room, "exquisitely panelled and papered," for ladies.[10] In addition, the club was available, with the permission of Carr, for meetings, concerts, lectures, and parties. A member could reserve the club for a private party for a fee of five pounds. There was a large room with a stage to accommodate the Amateur Dramatic Club's offerings, concerts, and dances. An excerpt from an account in the Acton paper of the club's annual dinner held on 25 February 1882 illustrates the return that club members got for their money. Two hundred guests assembled at the club for the dinner and were served the following:

Menu
Potages
Faussee Tortue liée
Consommé a la Brunoise
Poissons
Fillets de Soles aux fines herbes
Blanchaille frite et à la Diable
Entrees
Ris de Veau à la Jardiniere
Salmis de Coz de Bruyere aux Olives
Relevés
Poulet à la Bechamel
Langue de Boeuf
Selle de Mouton rôtie, Légumes
Salade à la Franciase

Entrements
Pouding à la Bedford
Creme à la Vanille
Pâtisseries Genoise glacée
Croutes d'Anchois à l'Indienne[11]

Jonathan Carr presided over the dinner and several informal speeches and toasts were given afterward. Since the speeches are so indicative of the aims and atmosphere of the community, it seems worthwhile to quote the account in the Acton newspaper:

Lord Colin Campbell said that his connection with Bedford Park had led him to suppose that it was an institution having this remarkable peculiarity—that it was bent upon reforming and remodelling every institution which belongs to the British (hear, hear), and amongst others the institution of after dinner speeches. . . . The duty which he had to perform, however, was of a most agreeable nature, as he had to ask them to drink to this toast— "Prosperity to the institutions of Bedford Park." Amongst those institutions, the first to which he would direct their attention was the Club, which seemed to have the remarkable peculiarity of parading the feelings of a great countryman of his, John Stuart Mill, who wrote a treatise upon the subjection of what was, after all, the stronger sex (laughter). . . . The next institution he should mention was the School of Art (applause). He had been told that it had progressed so far that even now it numbered no less than 250 pupils. Some people ridiculed the tendencies of Bedford Park, but he trusted that the School of Art would supply members for the Royal Academy (applause). [After toasting the Dramatic Club and the Athletic Club in the same vein] The noble lord then went on to say that he had obtained permission to name one institution which, perhaps, they might not have expected him to name—and that institution was that of his worthy friend, Mr. Carr (applause). It seemed almost impossible to enumerate the institutions of Bedford Park without naming him. It was unnecessary for him (the speaker) to dwell on the praises of Mr. Carr, as they had already been sung in a journal which he, for one, always read, *The St. James Gazette* (laughter). He believed it was the prevailing opinion that Bedford Park had the advantage of possessing a man of undoubted energy, under whose influence Bedford Park was likely to live and prosper (applause). With much pleasure he gave them the toast of "The institutions of Bedford Park."

Moncure Conway responded to this toast, the chairman next proposed a toast to "The Visitors." Mr. Passmore Edwards, M. P., responded to this toast:

> . . . He was not sure that Bedford Park was not the admiration of society, and that it appeared to be the "green spot of the world." . . . The speaker then spoke of Mr. Carr as a Herculean man who was a wonder in himself. He (Mr. Edwards) was speaking to a statesman the other day, and Bedford Park was mentioned, and the statesman expressed the opinion that Mr. Carr could say enough in ten minutes to tie the hands of the legislature for ten years (laughter).
>
> "The worship of the sunflower" was the last toast submitted, and the company then promenaded the rooms until shortly after eleven o'clock, when they dispersed.[12]

Lord Colin Campbell's reference to the *St. James Gazette* is, of course, a reference to the infamous "Ballad of Bedford Park" (see Appendix A, p. 123). His mention of Mill's treatise "On the Subjection of Women" stems from the Bedford Park Club's extraordinary practice of extending complete equality to women.

The variety of entertainments, many at the club, that was offered to the residents of Bedford Park can be seen in the *Gazette's* calendar for a fairly typical month, January, 1884:

January
7. Monday, 6 to 10 P.M.—Second Children's Ball, at the Club; tickets for children, 1s. 6d; for adults 2s. 6d.
10. Thursday, 3:30 P.M.—Lecture on "Botany," at the School of Art.
14. Monday, 8:30 P.M.—Annual Meeting of the Lawn Tennis Club, at the Club.

15.   Tuesday, 8:30 P.M.—Lecture on "The Older Edda, and Our Forefathers' Poetry," by Mr. York Powell, at the Club.

17.   Thursday, 8:00 P.M.—Meeting of the Bedford Park Liberal Association, at the Chiswick Club, High-road, Chiswick.

19.   Saturday, 8:00 P.M.—Meeting of the Natural History and Gardening Society, at the Club.

22.   Tuesday, 8:30 P.M.—Lecture on "the Younger Edda, and our Forefathers' Religion," by Mr. York Powell, at the Club.

25.   Friday, 8:30 P.M.—Dance at the Club; tickets (on sale before January 18), 3s. 6d.

26.   Saturday, 8:00 P.M.—Bedford Park Reunion, at the Club.

29.   Tuesday, 8:30 P.M.—Lecture on "The Sagas and Our Forefathers' Novels," by Mr. York Powell, at the Club.

31.   Thursday, 3:30 P.M.—Lecture on "Botany" by Professor Bentley, at the School of Art.[13]

The Second Children's Ball, held on 7 January, was indicative of the interest in children in Bedford Park, a place that provided that ideal of parents in every age: a good place to bring up children. There were frequent evenings for children. For example, on New Year's Eve, 1880, there was a Children's Evening at the club which included a performance of marionettes, a comic pantomime, Offenbach's "Lischen and Frischen," and a conjuring seance. A Children's Fancy Dress Ball was held on 30 December 1881, and it became an annual event. Another entertainment for children was provided by writing or adapting children's plays for them to perform to audiences of other children and doting parents at the club. These were made topical by writing names and institutions in Bedford Park into the texts.

Although none happens to be on the calendar printed for January 1884, the favorite type of party in Bedford Park seems to have involved dressing up; people especially enjoyed masquerades and fancy dress balls. This is the way Moncure Conway remembered a costume ball which took place in July 1880.

The grounds . . . were overhung with Chinese lanterns, and the swhard and bushes were lit up, as it were, with many-tinted giant glow-worms. The *fête champêtre* and the mirth of the ballroom went on side by side, with only a balcony and its luxurious cushions between them. Comparatively few of the ladies sought to represent any particular "character": there were about two hundred present and fancy costumes for both sexes were *de rigueur*; yet amongst all these there were few conventionally historical or allegorical characters. There was a notable absence of ambitious and costly dresses. The ladies had indulged their own tastes in design and color, largely assisted, no doubt, by the many artists which Bedford Park can boast, and the result was decidedly the most beautiful scene of the kind I have ever witnessed.

After the party, some young gentlemen, having danced until 5:00 A.M. decided to have a game of tennis and were still playing in their costumes at 8:00 A.M. when the tradesmen arrived. The latter, however, according to Conway, were so accustomed to odd behavior in Bedford Park that the costumes attracted little or no attention (see fig. 25).[14]

The botany lectures on the January calendar were in a series offered under the auspices of the London Society for the Extension of University courses. They were not nearly so popular as the series of Conversational Lectures of which York Powell's talks on Norse literature formed one unit. These used the talent in Bedford Park and encouraged discussion by the audience. Others in the series of Conversational Lectures were three each by James Sime on Goethe, Dr. Gordon Hogg on physiology, and Dr. John Todhunter on Italian Art. The *Gazette* emphasized that these lectures were prepared and delivered free of charge by the lecturers who looked for no other reward than the satisfaction of their audience.

Perhaps the most characteristic institution in Bedford Park was the Bedford Park Reunion, shown on the calendar for 26 January. The favorite occupation in Bedford Park was talk: formal debate, friendly discussion, any kind of communication seems to have been sought and the Reunion, begun in June 1882, was a society which met monthly for discussing social questions. The meetings were informal, according to the *Gazette* and aimed not so much at being debates as friendly discussions "in a drawing room."[15] The Reunion was designed to give residents an opportunity to present their ideas on questions of intellectual and social importance. The Reunion met on the last Saturday of each month and began with a prepared paper that led to open discussion. This list of the Reunion's discussion topics during its first year of existence lets us know what people were talking about in Bedford Park in 1882 and 1883.

1882

June 3, "The Relation of Women to the State"; introduced by James Sime

July 1, "The Influence of Drama upon Society"; Rev. J. W. Horsley

July 29, "The Education of the Young"; Miss Eliza Orme

August 26, "Compulsory Vaccination"; Arthur Young

September 30, "Capital Punishment"; Moncure Conway

October 28, "Is an Established Church Advantageous to the State?"; Dr. Gordon Hogg

November 25, "Dress Reform"; Mrs. Lynch

December 16, "The Literature of the Nursery"; Mrs. John Todhunter

1883

January 27, "The Harm Aestheticism has done to the Spread of Art"; J. T. Carr

February 24, "Home Rule"; G. H. Orpen

March 31, "Corporal Punishment"; Moncure Conway

April 28, "The Land Question"; Atherley Jones

May 26, "That the solution of the present difficulty regarding women's need of remunerative employment lies in the throwing open to all, without distinction of sex, the industries and profes-

sions hitherto monopolised by men," Miss Mary Eliza Richardson
June 3, Continuation of the discussion begun on May 26
June 30, "Is our holding of India beneficial to the Empire?"
Fox Bourne[16]

This rather remarkable list includes most of the problems of human beings as social creatures. The meetings gave the participants an opportunity to air their opinions and hear those of others on the relations between the sexes and the relations of the individual to the state (26 May, 3 June), the relations between the state and religion (28 October), the relations between state and empire (24 February, 30 June), individual freedom (26 August, 25 November, 26 May, 3 June), crime and punishment (30 September, 31 March), education (29 July, 16 December), art (1 July, 27 January) and the question of productive use and distribution of land (28 April). One must remember that these discussions did not take place in the usual meeting-hall atmosphere where the topic can be put aside when the speeches and discussion by an audience are over. The intellectual stimulation could be sustained for days in Bedford Park as people met casually in club, church, stores, pub, and on the tennis courts, not to mention casual meetings in the street. These were the burning topics of the day, and they were taken seriously. To get the flavor of public opinion in Bedford Park it is useful to follow the discussions on a selected topic, and, since it is once again a timely subject, the question of women's rights seems a good choice.

It is indicative of the "advanced" atmosphere at Bedford Park that five of the Reunion's discussions were led by women and four treat specific problems of women; this also reflects controversy in British society as a whole, because tremendous efforts were being made in the early 1880s to get women's suffrage included in the Third Reform

Bill. But Bedford Park was an oasis in the desert of Victorian prejudice against women, as in so many other things, and this enlightened attitude had practical application there, in the club.

Moncure Conway said of it, "It is speaking moderately to say it [the club] is as pure a sample of civilization as any institution upon this planet. After claiming that, my reader need hardly be informed that in it ladies and gentlemen are on a perfect equality."[17] The American journalist and poet Helen Hunt Jackson, writing on Bedford Park as "A New Utopia" for *The Boston Daily Advertiser*, remarked that the club was probably the only institution of its kind in the world —where there was no sex discrimination and where "any woman who lives in Bedford Park may go to the club, read periodicals, play billiards, smoke (if she likes) as freely as if she were a man."[18] Surely Bedford Park would be a fruitful place to listen to a public dialogue on the rights of women, but to get a proper perspective on the general atmosphere in which the dialogue takes place, it is necessary to remind oneself that as late as 1882 men were still seriously debating whether women could be expected to be intellectually equal to men because, after all, their brains are smaller.[19] Besides this rather doubtful physical handicap, women had a genuinely undeniable handicap where legal problems were concerned. For example, by Common Law the legal existence of women during marriage was suspended by being merged with that of their husbands. The Married Women's Property Act had been designed to promote equality between married women and single women, not between married women and men. In other words, its function was to keep a woman from being worse off, in questions of property, by marrying than she would be if she stayed single. Women could legally be awarded medical and law degrees, but they had first to be accepted at the appropriate professional school, which was no easy matter. The-oretically they could hold any office to which they could be legally appointed or elected, provided that the duties of that office could be performed by a male deputy. This meant that theoretically a woman could be sheriff; practically, it meant nothing at all and served simply as a specious argument to justify the monopoly of males in appointive and elective offices. It was true in theory only because there were no precedents. Women could not vote for members of parliament, although outside London single women could vote in some municipal and school elections.[20] These circumstances make the amount and quality of discussion about women's rights in Bedford Park truly remarkable.

The circumstances surrounding the eventual granting of women's suffrage can be understood more easily in the light of discussions such as those in Bedford Park, for one of the great enigmas is *how* women ever gained the right to vote, since it had to be granted by men. The answer, of course, lies in the fact that they had the support of some reasonable men. Bedford Park had its share of these rea-sonable men who favored equal opportunities and rights for women, but it also had its share of men who thought woman's place was in the home and a number of women who agreed with them. The remarkable thing was the amount of public debate in which each side was allowed to speak and to be listened to.

The question of women's rights was first discussed at a Reunion on 3 June 1882. Moncure Conway chaired the meeting and introduced James Sime, an authority on Les-sing and Goethe who lived in the Park, who spoke strongly in favor of extending the franchise to women because he felt that any class which is unrepresented is neglected. However, he deplored the damage done to the cause by the "exaggerated" language of some of its supporters. He was

followed by a suffragette named Lydia Becker who con-
tended that it would be impossible to exaggerate when describing the condition of some married women. She felt
that women were better qualified to legislate some matters
than men because they know more about them. The usual
arguments were presented that women were not given equal
employment opportunities because they were not competent
to perform certain duties, and in response to a certain
amount of bullying Miss Becker felt compelled to point
out that she had not come to be cross-examined. The last
blow was struck by a doctor who introduced the indefensible
but unanswerable accusation of "abnormality" into the
discussion:

> Dr. Beckingsale remarked that an essential and innate difference
> existed between the sexes, as much marked mentally as physi-
> cally—that whereas man was mainly distinguished by the poses-
> sion of the reflective faculties, woman, the normal woman, was
> characterized by the possession of the intuitive, perceptive, and
> emotional qualities, qualities which did not fit them for the ex-
> ercise of the franchise, and indeed, few women who were
> genuinely feminine displayed the slightest aptitude for, or in-
> terest in, politics.[21]

This was the last point of the evening, few women being
willing to adopt the label of abnormality by defending their
interest in politics!

On 25 November 1883, the Reunion again took up a problem especially interesting to women: dress reform. For this
they called in the president and secretary of the Rational
Dress Society, the Viscountess Harberton (Florence Pomeroy) and a Mrs. Lynch. They used charts and diagrams to
illustrate the folly and danger to health of tight lacing and
supported their plea for sensible dress with letters from William Morris and Alfred Gotch. Lady Harberton modeled a

"dual costume" which could be either a long dress that was shortened by unbuttoning a bottom section just below the knee or a divided skirt. In a pamphlet published by the Rational Dress Society in 1885 she recommended divided skirts as an alternative to the prevailing style that, with its pinched waists and heavy skirts, sinned "against Art, Health, and Utility." She claimed that stays caused disease by displacing organs; lifting and dragging heavy skirts (a weight of six pounds on each knee as a woman climbed stairs) was absolutely debilitating. "The constant burden of a cumbrous dress enslaves the mind in the same proportion as it weakens physical vigour. All tinkering and patching of the old system is vain. What we require is a fresh start."[22] Two men at the meeting felt compelled to say that they found the costume modeled by Lady Harberton ugly and impractical. But the facts cited by the speaker made a strong impression on the audience.[23]

These first two discussions of women's problems and rights were marked by a fair amount of restraint on the part of the women; but on 26 May 1883, when women's rights were again the topic under consideration, the lid on their reticence blew off. This time when challenged and provoked they answered back. The introductory speaker, Miss Mary Eliza Richardson, member of the London School Board and proprietor of the Bedford Park Stores, was an outspoken advocate of equality for women, and the topic that she developed on this occasion started a fight that had to be carried over to another meeting of the Reunion. Her theme was "that the solution of the present difficulty regarding women's need of remunerative employment lies in the throwing open to all, without distinction of sex, the industries and professions hitherto monopolized by men." The proceedings of this meeting fill a full column of space in the Acton paper. Miss Richardson's account was witty and incisive; she began by noting that while there were many more women in England than men, and the disparity in numbers was growing, the only jobs open to women were those of governess, school mistress, and telegraph and post office clerks. This took her into the main body of her argument.

> Miss Richardson then read an abstract from Adam Smith's "Wealth of Nations," and said that what Smith said of man she held to be equally true of woman. Woman was right in attempting by whatever way she could to get to the top of the tree, and her interest should rest between herself and her employer alone. . . . If women must work, who was competent to say what they were to do? Was the sphere of woman to be marked out by Act of Parliament? Women claimed the right to do whatever they could. Did they find it necessary to pass an Act of Parliament to prevent weak men being blacksmiths? (laughter). . . . She was not speaking against the men as a class, but she wished to point out that there were many things the women could do, although they could not perform the hardest work now done by men. Miss Richardson concluded her admirable paper by stating that at least fair play and no favour should be shown to her sex.[24]

The response was immediate and exhaustive. Mr. Mosenier, a native of Calcutta, affirmed that the throwing open of factory jobs to women in India had not been morally degrading to them; however, he had to admit that he personally preferred "shy and retiring" Indian as well as English ladies. Mr. Foote said that while he agreed with the abstract principle involved in Miss Richardson's argument, the fact was that the professions were already overcrowded; to throw them open to women too would only result in more misery. Then Miss Richardson found a champion:

> Miss Orme, with withering scorn, then rode into the area of debate, on the hobby horse of herself and the fair and learned opener of the discussion and smote the last speaker hip and thigh,

searching, however, not very successfully, for a gap in his logical armour, wherein to pierce him through and through. . . . Miss Orme almost fiercely attributed equally selfish and ill-concerned motives to her predecessor in the debate, and urged him and others to look round and see the numbers of women whose only possible opening was the occupation of ill-paid governesses or the worse alternative of unsympathetic matrimonial alliance, and concluded a sufficiently spirited address by a warm eulogy of lady doctors; an emphatically expressed opinion that most ladies would prefer to consult lady solicitors; and a renewed expression of disgust at the shortsighted selfishness of the employers of labour in disregarding the claims of the willing women-workers of the industrial class.

This strong speech was followed by a male supporter of the women, who, according to the paper, depended on quotations from Tennyson and George Eliot rather than reason for his argument. He, in turn, brought forth a biting speech by Mr. Atherley Jones who felt that women had not taken advantage of the trades and professions open to them. For example, while it was perfectly true that they were barred from the ministry in the Church of England, they were free to become Dissenting Ministers, and they could show their sincerity by doing so. Furthermore, "He ventured to say, amid cheers and hisses, that every lady there would prefer to be attended in sickness by a male doctor, and declared he knew of only one lady doctor who was at all generally recognized by the members of her own profession." A woman brought the debate to a close with a plea that the law of evolution be allowed to work in this case. Throw all employment open to women, she thought, and the fittest would survive; those who tried to do what they were not capable of doing would perish. The evening ran out before the audience was satisfied, so they agreed to meet one week later to continue.[25]

So, on 3 June 1883 they went at it again. On this occa-

sion another familiar creature appeared, The Woman Who
Is Happy with Her Lot.

> Miss Danvers then made some remarks from a carefully prepared
> paper, in which she supported the prevalent and popular idea of
> the sphere and objects of woman's work, and expressed dislike
> to any revolutionary changes (hear, hear) regarding women's
> proper sphere as the domestic hearth, and her mission in the
> world in which she had shone in all ages and in all parts of the
> world.

But this did not reflect the feelings of the audience; people
had had time to think, and there was now more support than
adverse criticism for Miss Richardson's original proposition.
Two prepared statements in favor of it were followed by remarks from the floor. Four of the most respected men in the
community spoke strongly in favor of the motion: the local
physician, Dr. Gordon Hogg, gave his opinion that women
would make excellent doctors, and he felt that popular
prejudice as well as legal restraints should be removed from
their aspirations. He thought that although there had not
been as many female as there had been male geniuses, most
professions did not require genius anyway. J. T. Carr recommended that women not rest until they were usefully employed in all walks of life; they must not be selective but must
be actively competitive for *all* positions. Moncure Conway
maintained that women were indeed as capable of genius as
men but had been held back by their inferior educational
opportunities. James Sime advocated giving women a fair
trial.

> Miss Richardson then replied, and thanked the speakers who had
> so cordially supported her cause. She instanced as one sign of the
> times the increasing number of women who mounted to the tops
> of omnibuses (laughter) but said that for her part, although she

had even aspired as high as this, she still felt that the cumbrous garb of woman, which she devoutly hoped might be soon improved away (a laugh) had formed an insuperable obstacle to her aspirations in that direction.[26]

However heartwarming the support of gentlemen on these occasions must have been, it appears not to have been totally satisfactory, for within a month of this meeting the ladies formed their own group, the Ladies' Discussion Society. Although the minutes of the club are not available, it is obvious from accounts in the newspapers that it was no neighborhood sewing circle. These women approached the grave problems facing them with the determination and attitudes familiar to present-day women's liberation groups.

Membership was open to all interested women, whether residents of Bedford Park or not. This allowed a spicier mixture than purely local membership could have provided, and the society attracted some of the most vocal feminists in England as well as guests like the famous American suffragette, Elizabeth Cady Stanton. The Ladies' Discussion Society met monthly, except for August, September, and December, on a Saturday afternoon at 2:00 at The Orchard, the home of Miss Eliza Orme.

The formation of a discussion society restricted to women drew interested reaction in the press. *The Bedford Park Gazette* thought it a laudable scheme that the ladies have a place to discuss matters without being bullied, as they sometimes were at the Reunion. *The Whitehall Review* saw it differently:

We all know what an amazing amount of superfluous energy the ordinary human tongue is capable of disposing, but what shall we say when we hear that in Bedford Park the female tongue has been publicly unloosed, for the ladies have started a discussion society of their own![27]

97

In February 1884, when the ladies had been meeting for eight months, *The Bedford Park Gazette* ran a letter from a member's husband begging the editor to use his influence in getting the ladies to meet on a day other than Saturday when a man could reasonably, he thought, expect to enjoy the company of his wife. The March 1884 issue of the *Gazette* noted that appeals had been made that the debates in the ladies' society be printed in full. They never were, and throughout the known existence of the society men kept on expressing their contempt, as in the following letter which appeared in the Acton paper signed by "An Admirer of the Neatly Darned Stocking."

Gentlemen's Discussion Society

Sir, On the 15th inst. the following announcement reached me by postcard of the opening session of the above society. . . . The winter session of the Bedford Park Discussion Society commences on December 20, at the house of Hon. Secretary. The question under discussion will be "Stocking Darning" and "How to Make a Beefsteak Pudding." Members are requested to be punctual, as the discussion cannot be prolonged over two hours, many of the members having to retire early in order to wash the children and put them to bed. . . . the Gentlemen's Discussion Society, perhaps, will do some good and direct, if not the attention of the ladies to the usefulness of these humble acts, at least show the gentlemen the advantage of becoming proficient therein themselves, and so enable their wives, daughters, and sisters to withdraw their large minds from such simple handiwork, and set them at liberty to discuss and devote their time and high capacities to the more important subject of state affairs, both home and foreign. As to nursing children, the gentlemen will easily fall into the duties consequent thereon now that they are relieved of their public obligations by personages whom we all value and admire.[28]

Certainly not oblivious to such scorn, though apparently not influenced by it either, the ladies in the discussion society continued to meet in ever-growing numbers, and they continued to meet on Saturdays. It is interesting that they considered again some of the questions which had been discussed at the Reunion; possibly they felt that in the presence of men they had not been able to say all they wanted to. The meetings followed the same pattern as the Reunion, a prepared paper led to discussion. In the first year they discussed the following topics:

1883

July, "The Education of Girls"; Miss Novelli

October, "The Education of Boys"; Mrs. Fox Bourne [This paper was written by Elizabeth Cady Stanton who had been present at the first meeting but was unable to attend this one to read her paper.]

November, "Dress Reform"; Mrs. Lynch [Again Lady Harberton was present to take part in the discussion.]

1884

January, "State Interference"; Mrs. G. H. Orpen

February, "Vegetarianism,"; Mrs. James Sime

March, "The Advisability of women studying science and the opportunities for them to do so"; Mrs. Henry May

April, "The Advantage of women having debating societies of their own at which they can practice the art of public speaking"; Miss Mary Eliza Richardson

May, "The general belief in the inferiority of women is not based on evidence"; Mrs. Charles MacLaren

June, "Domestic Servants"; Mrs. Keith and Mrs. Cockerell

July, "A comparison between different vocations open to women."

The most interesting discussion was probably the one held in May; Laura MacLaren, a second-generation suffragette, was wife of the Radical member of parliament Charles MacLaren. *The Bedford Park Gazette* gave its usual cryptic notice.

. . . Mrs. Charles MacLaren presided, and read an exhaustive paper on the proposition that the general belief in the inferiority of women is not based upon evidence. She treated the subject under the three heads of the physical, intellectual, and moral qualities of men and women. Mrs. Orpen spoke in opposition, and the discussion was continued by Mrs. Sime, Mrs. Trautschold, Miss Orme, and Miss Woods. The motion was finally carried by a majority of four.[29]

Mrs. MacLaren evidently called a spade a spade, for the effect on that most diaphanous of all substances, the male ego, was evident in the same issue of the *Gazette*. The ladies' discussion moved the Outsider to publish these remarks:

I know nothing, of course, of what was said and done the other day at the meeting of your Ladies' Discussion Society, to which it seems that none but those who wear petticoats, or perhaps, "divided skirts" are admitted, and at which, I doubt not, much good sense, with an average amount of nonsense, was talked in support of the oddly-worded proposition "that the common belief in the inferiority of women to men is not based upon evidence.

One wonders what he found odd in the wording; at any rate, he was interested in the proceedings. He goes on to say that women in Bedford Park, by their participation in sports, dramatics, debates, and by the rout of two male opponents at a local suffrage meeting had pretty well proved Mrs. MacLaren's thesis. He himself had always favored women's rights and looked forward to the day when they would have the vote. However, there was one area in which they tended to show themselves inferior, and this was in the area of snobbishness. Men in Bedford Park were more cosmopolitan than women; they all associated freely with each other while the women did not. Women sneered at women who worked for a living as actresses or governesses, or who carried their babies on walks instead of employing nursemaids, or who didn't go to church, and so forth. In *this* instance, he said, "The common belief in the inferiority of women to men *is* based upon evidence."[30]

If the Outsider thought he could get away with using women's provincialism, which in their opinions stemmed from male oppression, as a jawbone to beat them with, he had only to wait for the next issue of the *Gazette* to learn his mistake. It carried a letter from a lady who said that she had not met any of the snobbishness he mentioned, although she had done several of the things for which, according to him, she should have been snubbed in Bedford Park. She explained that the women's lack of "cosmopolitanism," which he was able to discern in men, resulted from women having to be more careful about their acquaintances than men. Lacking clubs in which to mingle freely, they could cultivate only those acquaintances whom they felt free to entertain at home. Her letter was bitingly sarcastic in places and indicated that the female pen as well as the female tongue had been loosed in Bedford Park.

> . . . "An Outsider" admits that "men are not perfect" in cosmopolitanism; I will go further, and say that their example is not one that we should wish to follow, and it seems to me that he might find as wide a scope for his missionary enthusiasm among men as he could in showing his "chicken-hearted and purblind sisters" what he thinks they ought to be and do. Were the aspirations which he feels on rare occasions and in self-sacrificing moods fulfilled, "An Outsider's" opinion as to what women ought to be and do could not possibly remain what it is at present.[31]

The letter was signed "Fair Play." The editor regretted that there was no opportunity for the Outsider to reply. We are left suspended, for this was the last issue of *The Bedford*

Park Gazette. The only reference after this to the Ladies' Discussion Society is a notice in the 4 July 1885 issue of the Acton paper which notes that the Society is still very active with a membership numbering over one hundred. However, the following article is a tribute to the spirit of the Bedford Park women, who seem to have progressed a bit further than the "dual costume" although they had been left out of the Third Reform Bill in 1884.

> The New Woman Is Asserting Herself at Chiswick
> The other day, writes a well known Chiswick schoolmaster, one of my boys was going to the cricket field in Bedford Park, when, in crossing the road, he was knocked down by a lady on a bicycle. As soon as the boy pulled himself together the lady made a rush at him, and taking him by the shoulders, gave him a good shaking and threatened to lock him up for *obstructing the thoroughfare!* When he came back to school I noticed that he was a bit upset and asked him what was the matter. He told me that a lady on a bicycle had knocked him down. I asked him who the lady was, and his reply was, "Please, sir, I don't know; but she was a lady in trousers." Comment is needless.[32]

The local preoccupation with good talk was not confined to the public forums like the Bedford Park Reunion and The Ladies' Discussion Society. During the 1880s and 1890s there was a private conversation club of twelve selected gentlemen which, at one time or another, included some of the best talkers in England. This club, founded by Moncure Conway about 1882, was called the Calumet, after the North American Indian ceremony of the peace pipe. It met alternate Sundays in rotation at the members' homes and lasted from 9:00 P.M. until it ended naturally—sometimes at 3:00 A.M. In the early years the Calumet is known to have included Conway, James Sime, John Todhunter, Gordon Hogg, G. H. Orpen, York Powell, Fox Bourne, and

Jonathan Carr. In later years it boasted John Butler Yeats, R. A. M. Stevenson, and Oliver Elton. The quality of conversation in the club can be judged by the reputations of some of its members.

The last quarter of the nineteenth century had a number of men who excelled in talk, including W. E. Henley and Oscar Wilde. John Butler Yeats was said to be equal to these, and R. A. M. Stevenson took the laurel from them all. Stevenson did other things for a living; he was for years art critic of the *Pall Mall Gazette*, tried painting and even taught it, wrote books on Velasquez and Rubens (it is characteristic that he thought Rubens had gone out of favor because fat women were no longer in style), but talk was his real career and greatest gift. In his autobiography H. G. Wells relates that he tried to graft Stevenson's style of talk onto Ewart in *Tono Bungay* but felt that he had achieved only a pale copy of what Stevenson could do. He is the "Spring-Heel'd Jack" in his cousin Robert Louis Stevenson's essay "Talk and Talkers." But Stevenson was only one member of the Calumet; while the others were not so famed for talk as he, there were several who could hold their own. One of these, of course, was John Butler Yeats, whose style was much admired by G. K. Chesterton for its spontaneity in which words were arranged like lightning:

A long and elaborately balanced sentence, with dependent clauses alternative or antithetical, would flow out of such talkers with every word falling into place quite as immediately and innocently as most people would say it was a fine day or a funny business in the papers. I can still remember old Yeats, that graceful greybeard, saying in an offhand way about the South African War, "Mr. Joseph Chamberlain has the character, as he has the face, of a shrewish woman who ruins her husband by extravagance; and Lord Salisbury has the character, as he has the face, of the man who is so ruined."[33]

103

It is amusing to imagine an evening at the Calumet if politics should have come up. John Butler Yeats and John Todhunter were Irish Nationalists, and Yeats was pro-Boer as well. York Powell was "socialist jingo" and imperialist to the core, while Fox Bourne, who had been born in Jamaica, was for years secretary of the Aborigines Protection Society and devoted to alleviating the suffering of natives victimized by colonialism. Whenever the Irish Nationalist leader John O'Leary was in town he was invited to come to the Calumet, and, according to Oliver Elton, O'Leary was one man who could terrify every one of them, no matter what political sympathies they had. There were apparently times, however, when his claws remained sheathed. This is from a letter of Yeats in 1901:

> O'Leary was here on Sunday and was in great form. The Calumets were delighted—he discoursed the whole time with great astuteness, avoiding dangerous subjects. He is not without the wisdom of the serpent. I tried several times to roll in the apple of discord, but they all looked as if they did not see it. O'Leary told me that not for twenty years has he been so happy as this war has made him.[34]

The members of the Calumet were mostly nonreligious, and the following quotation describes a discussion that they had in the early eighties on the question of disestablishment of the Anglican Church. Conway's own view, with which the group concurred, was this:

> He [the clergyman] is there for the culture of the country, for the humanities—a scholar and a gentleman—and if his Church were disestablished, reduced to a mere sect in competition with vulgar sectarians, the clergyman would not be there. . . . Disestablishment would be like the toppling down of lighthouses on rough moral coasts. As for the creeds and formulas, they have no more effect on the masses than if they were in Latin; they offend only

104

the few that can understand them; altogether, with the music and the responses they make a pretty Sunday concert. It is the refinement and the benevolence of the clergyman and his family that practically make his gospel. . . . All agreed that our free thinking societies were performing a necessary function in criticizing the creeds, enlightening educated people, and thus surrounding the Church with restraints on clericalism and assisting its broad and tolerant wing.[35]

It is worth noting that this rather astonishing statement is from the pen of a Unitarian minister who had begun as a Methodist and worked his way to this position through prayer (until he stopped believing in it) and deep soul searching. It is also easy to imagine the dissension that might surface at any time in a closely knit community which harbored these freethinkers as well as the ritualists at Saint Michael and All Angels.

Another famous member of the Calumet was Sergius Stepniac, the Russian emigré nihilist. In fact, the Calumet members were among the last to talk with him, for they met at his house on the evening before he was killed at the level crossing in Bedford Park on 24 December 1895.

Although the talk in Bedford Park provided background for everything else, other things were going on as well. The Music Society gave performances and sponsored others by professional musicians. The reporter from the Acton paper was impressed by the pleasantly relaxed atmosphere at concerts. The prettiness of the little auditorium and the familiarity of members of the audience with each other and frequently with the performers too gave the impression that music was being performed among friends in a gracious drawing room.

The Amateur Dramatic Club was extremely active, producing three or four plays a year, usually farces and melodramas or *tableaux vivants*. On several occasions the Dramatic Club

produced plays written by a Bedford Park resident, acted
by residents, with sets and costumes designed and executed
by local artists. The most important one of these, and, indeed,
perhaps the most significant performance ever done in Bedford Park, was John Todhunter's pastoral play, *A Sicilian
Idyl*. This play was important not for its literary merits, but
because of the connection with it of William Butler Yeats
and the consequent effect on him. For Willy, as he was
known in Bedford Park, had talked Todhunter into writing
the play. Yeats was interested in avoiding the realism of the
contemporary theater, and having seen the George Macdon-
ald family perform a dramatized version of *Pilgrim's Progress*
in that very theater before a backdrop of calico hangings,
he reasoned that the best way to get the effect he wanted
was to produce a poetical drama with simple backdrops instead of realistic settings. Nobody would expect thrills from
a pastoral, so Todhunter should avoid every oratorical phrase
and cadence and concentrate on achieving true poetic drama.
He had himself begun *The Countess Cathleen* with this idea
in mind. Todhunter seems to have been ready to follow
Yeats's suggestions, and in May of 1890 the community was
busy with the production. Yeats, who wrote literary gossip
for the *Boston Pilot*, described the bustle in his column. His
attitude toward the community is as interesting as the production he is describing:

> Dr. Todhunter, of Trinity College, Dublin, has written a charming
> little pastoral drama, called *A Sicilian Idyl*, and founded on a story
> in Theocritus. He is bringing it out at the little club theatre here,
> in the redbricked and redtiled suburb, Bedford Park, where so
> many of us writing people have gathered. . . . The whole play,
> with its graceful and many-colored Greek costumes, will make a
> charming unity with the quaint little theatre, with its black panels
> covered with gilt cupids. If successful . . . there is some talk of
> getting up an annual venture of this same kind, a sort of May Day

festival of dramatic poetry. What the play next year will be I cannot say, at present all concerned are deep in Arcadia. In every corner of Dr. Todhunter's study are shepherd crooks and long sticks topped with pine cones to serve as wands for shepherd priests of Bacchus who in the first scene enter in slow procession carrying the image of the god and singing his praises, and on the chairs are colored silks to be made into stately costumes.[36]

The play was a sellout to twice the number of performances they had planned to have. People came from all over London, and Yeats enthusiastically reported the affair to his Boston readers.

It has been acted three times—Monday, Wednesday, and Friday last—at the little club theatre in Bedford Park, and will be again next Saturday preliminary to its possible revival elsewhere. The long room with its black panels and gilt cupids has been crowded with really distinguished audiences.

On Friday I noticed Miss Alma Murray, the creator of the part of Beatrice in the Shelley Society's performance of *Cenci*; Miss Winifred Emery, now performing in Buchanan's *Tam Bay*; Mr. Cyril Maude; Mr. Terriss, just returned for a time to the Lyceum fold; and Lady Archibald Campbell, of pastoral drama celebrity; and among social and literary notables, Mrs. Jopling Rowe; Miss Mathilde Blind, whose translation of Marie Bashkirtseff's Diary is making such a stir just now; Mrs. Charles Hancock, of the Women's Liberal Association; Mr. Theodore Watts the critic; and Miss May Morris.[37]

The acting was done by a combination of local amateurs and a few professionals hired for this occasion. The amateurs, paced by Florence Farr and Heron Allen, were much more impressive to Yeats than the professionals; they read poetry for pleasure, and this was apparent in the way they said their lines; they made no attempt to act; and while they were on the stage they held all the attention. Their very speech was music and lent a nobility to the poetry according to Yeats, who said, years later, that these performances of *A Sicilian Idyl* taught him that in producing drama that depends upon the beauty of language, poetical culture can be more important than professional experience.[38] He also took from that experience one of the informing principles of his later career in the theater, the idea that theatrical art is not necessarily meant for popular consumption: "We must make a theatre for ourselves and our friends and for a few simple people who understand from sheer simplicity what we understand from scholarship and thought."[39] This was his intention with the later Irish National Theatre. He thought that a similar venture in pursuit of "pure" theater should be attempted with annual plays at Bedford Park. The success of the first venture, however, went to Todhunter's head. He produced *A Sicilian Idyl* in the commercial theater and did not follow through with the same type of thing the next year in Bedford Park.

This play was the first time Yeats had seen Florence Farr act, although he had made her acquaintance sometime before. She was sister-in-law to the Bedford Park resident H. M. Paget and lived only a short distance away in Brook Green. After their collaboration in the production of Todhunter's play, Yeats and Florence Farr became great friends; they began giving performances of chanted poetry to her accompaniment on the psaltery. She asked Yeats to write a play for her and her young niece, who was H. M. Paget's daughter. He complied with *The Land of Heart's Desire*, which was performed as a curtain raiser for G. B. Shaw's *Arms and the Man*.[40]

The interests of Bedford Park residents were not confined to literary and musical matters, as the Natural History and Gardening Society proved. The meetings of this club were extremely varied and, as in the case of many other local clubs, frequently ended with the floor being cleared for dancing. One of the first meetings, in October 1883, included an exhibition of flowers, butterflies, birds, fossils, and flower paintings as well as short addresses on sixteenth-century botanical works, birds shot by Dr. Gordon Hogg and Bowdler Sharpe during their holiday in Romney Marsh, fossil plants in the coal measures, beekeeping, and the eye of the bee and other insects.

Another popular pastime was tennis, and the Lawn Tennis Club held an annual tournament and sent its players to play in tournaments sponsored by other clubs. Mr. Carr provided and maintained excellent asphalt courts to be rented by the members of the tennis club; a fee of 10s. 6d. bought a member privileges for his family and guests for a year, while courts were rented by the hour. The Lawn Tennis Club was an active social center, and since very little happened in Bedford Park without controversy it is no surprise to find outraged letters to the editor of the Acton paper about the residents of Bedford Park playing tennis on Sunday—*all day* Sunday, in fact. The editorial comment presents the position of the paper on this weighty matter: "If lawn tennis on Sundays is right at the Bedford Park Club, may it not be claimed that billiards, bagatelle, bowls, and even skittles would be proper at the surrounding public houses and would be equally allowable. That is the legitimate outcome of such reasoning and surely every Englishman would deprecate such an influx of Sunday amusements!"[41] Moncure Conway recalled in his autobiography that the Sunday tennis play continued in spite of the efforts of the Reverend Mr. Wilson to get it banned during canonical hours. He had no objection to Sunday tennis except that it diminished his congregation, so he sent around a petition to have it limited to afternoon hours. The only people in Bedford Park who would sign the petition were Mr. and Mrs. Conway who did not object to the tennis games in the least but were afraid the controversy would result in getting all Sunday entertainment banned if the tennis players could not be prevailed upon to give up a few hours of play.

This brief account of the entertainments in Bedford Park shows that the residents always had something to do without leaving their own neighborhood. Two other amenities added to the sovereignty of the community and encouraged self-containment. These were the church, already mentioned in connection with its "high" services, and the stores.

The parish of Saint Michael and All Angels was constituted in December 1879 and included, in addition to Bedford Park, the part of the old parish of Chiswick "bounded by the Brentford-road on the south, Fishers' Lane, Turnham Green on the west, and Goldhawk-road, Hammersmith, on the east. The present population of the parish—which comprises a good many poor—is about 3500."[42] The church in Bedford Park was very active and at one time ran a soup kitchen in the parish hall for the poor.

The stores offered almost anything a resident could want in the way of goods and services. They were called *cooperative stores* misleadingly in that the cooperation was merely between the departments and referred to the business organization rather than to the cooperative principle.[43] The stores' advertisement in the July 1884, *Gazette* listed the following departments: grocery, provisions, butcher, fishmonger, poulterer, greengrocer, furnishing, fancy goods, coal, wine and spirit, china and glass, stationery, drug, turnery, ironmongery, house decorating, livery stables, and a post and telegraph office. The decorating department also undertook building, plumbing, and hot water fitting. The departments were served by a single cashier, and the whole enterprise seems like a giant protosupermarket. The stores were under the proprietorship of Miss Mary Eliza Richardson who ran the business through her manager, a man named

Slater, from their opening in 1879 until the original company went into liquidation in 1894. Another company took over the business at that time and ran it until sometime around the turn of the century.

The Tabard, of course, provided a pub, restaurant, and hotel. The scheme mentioned by Moncure Conway that involved a communal kitchen to provide meals for all who wanted to contract for them never materialized. It is remarkable that it was even discussed, but the Outsider thought it might be practical. A central kitchen would eliminate the necessity of heavy cooking in individual homes; he thought each family might order dinner from a daily menu and have it sent round in an iron hot-tray with separate compartments for fish, meat, and so forth. His suggestion for financing the venture is interesting, for it names the ways most things in Bedford Park were done: "It ought not to be difficult for such a kitchen to be started, either by a co-operative alliance between a number of inhabitants, or by one or two working alone and protected against the risk of loss by a guarantee or a subscription from a sufficient number of householders to cover working expenses."[44] If there was "co-operation" in Bedford Park it seems usually to have had a capitalistic basis.

Such, then, were the organizations and activities of Bedford Park. It is noteworthy that none of the institutions that gave the residents of Bedford Park so much pleasure were unique, with the possible exception of the Bedford Park Club. Most middle-class communities of the time had musical societies, amateur dramatic societies, and tennis clubs. What the other communities did not have was a sense of purpose and a sense of unity which allowed individuals to work for the common good: the search for "corporate happiness" in other words. At Bedford Park a number of people wanted the same things, and they had a center built into

111

the community for achieving them as well as leadership to
see them through. Bedford Park was too big by the middle
of the 1890s to retain the little "village ideals" of the early
community, but many of the institutions begun in the early
1880s lasted for years. A resident named William Brown,
writing an article on the club for the *Acton, Chiswick & Turnham Green Gazette* refers to Bedford Park as "that home of
aesthetic culture now fast being invaded by the Philistine,"
and lists the "social features" still enjoyed by club members:
a permanent and circulating library in connection with
Mudies; monthly dances with fancy costume balls at regular
intervals; Reunions once a month as well as a separate Club
Discussion Society; Natural History and Gardening Society;
Amateur Dramatic Club; Lawn Tennis Club with six grass
and two asphalt courts plus two other courts for children;
Musical Society; and Chess Club. The Bedford Park Club by
this time was the property of a small limited liability company made up by residents and was managed by a small
committee selected annually by the members. The membership numbered 200, and Mr. Brown invited new members to
join.[45]

In spite of the apparently thriving condition of the club,
the community at Bedford Park was doomed by this time;
and in 1896 the Acton paper ran this assessment from
Cassell's *Book of the Household* with its own comment.

". . . As all the earlier inhabitants of Bedford Park were drawn
together by mutual taste, there was a great deal of sociability
and pleasant interchange of ideas among them. With the con-
tinual laying out of new roads and building of more houses it has
rather outgrown its original character of a community, but still
there is a good deal of similarity among its inhabitants, many of
whom would be positively unhappy anywhere else." The accuracy
of the latter part of the notice quoted can be attested by anyone
who knows Bedford Park. It is rapidly outgrowing its original
bounds, the erection of houses and the laying out of new roads

entirely altering the appearance of some parts, the distinctive character of the residences not being maintained so rigidly as heretofore.[46]

Something about this tugs at the mind. There seems to have been such a connection between the community and the architectural style of the development that the community itself was violated by the building of less authentic Queen Anne houses just as surely as it was violated by an influx of people who did not share the interests of the original residents. One recalls, in this connection, editorial comment in the same paper sixteen years earlier that the main charm of the place came from its uniqueness—the combination of "cozy comfort," resulting from laying out the estate to accommodate necessity and comfort rather than fashion, with the characteristics of the Queen Anne Revival architecture which gave it unity.[47] This introduces the possibility that the failure of the early community may have resulted from the disintegration of those cohesive forces that brought it together in the first place. Aestheticism certainly went out of style, and the early leaders of the community were never replaced by younger, vigorous men of the same caliber. Perhaps there were other approaches to life by the mid-1890s, as there were different approaches to architecture evidenced by Voysey's solution of the problems of economy and comfort in the Forster house without resorting to Queen Anne Revival ornamentation for "cozy comfort." However this may be, the fact remains that for a while there was indeed a rich and satisfying community life amounting to "corporate happiness" at Bedford Park.

Chapter 5

BEDFORD PARK THROUGH THE YEARS

YEATS, CHESTERTON, AND BEDFORD PARK

Up to this point we have been dealing with contemporary accounts of the early years at Bedford Park. It remains now to deal with some well-known memories of life there and to bring the history up to the present.

The most famous accounts of Bedford Park stemming from memory are those of William Butler Yeats and G. K. Chesterton, and I have reserved comment on their opinions to avoid giving them undue emphasis, for to speak of Bedford Park in terms of Yeats and Chesterton would be to wag the dog by the tail. Although they are undoubtedly the most famous people ever connected with it, their success came later; when they were participants in the social and cultural life of the Park they were young and unknown. They were simply part of the life at Bedford Park which they both, in some measure, damn with faint praise in later years. Their activities there are interesting in the light of their later criticism, for they seem to have exemplified, as young men, those qualities they find most amusing in their later reflections on Bedford Park.

John Butler Yeats, William's father, moved his family to live in Bedford Park during two separate periods of time. They lived first at 8 Woodstock Road from 1876 until 1880, when they returned to Ireland. Then they came back to 3

Blenheim Road in March 1888, where the family household remained until about 1900.

At the time of the family's first move to Bedford Park, Willy was eleven years old. When they returned in 1888 he was twenty-three. John Butler Yeats preferred good company to anything else and lived in Bedford Park because he found the other residents congenial. He disliked the rest of Victorian life, which he considered to be crass and ugly, and Bedford Park was cheap enough for him to afford to live there.

William Butler Yeats recalls in *The Trembling of the Veil* that he was disappointed when the family moved back to Bedford Park in 1888. The charm was gone for him, and he indicates that it was gone for others also—the romantic illusions which had caused enthusiasm in the beginning had turned to exaggerated criticism of leaky roofs and bad drainage, criticism which he discounts. His harshest criticism is for the men who were friends of his father, men who did not like to work, had no ambition or ability to concentrate on anything that would make them successful, and were willing to put down whatever they were doing and talk. They seemed to him to be two removes from reality and incapable of amounting to much. They seem, from his account, to have been poseurs and dilettantes, and yet while he lived there he himself was not only very much part of the scene, he was considered a character. A letter to Kathryn Tynan shortly before the family's move in March 1888 shows what he anticipated in Bedford Park.

We go to our new house, 3 Blenheim Road, Bedford Park, on the 25th of this month; a fine roomy house, which by good luck we have got very cheap. Bedford Park is the least Londonish place hereabouts, a silent tree filled place where everything is a little idyllic, except the cockroaches that abound here. The quantity of new wood brings them and the old wood brings a stray nightin-

115

gale now and again, says rumour, and certainly thrushes and blackbirds in almost country plenty. I will have a study to myself with one of those white wooden balconies native to that part of the world.[1]

In 1889 he again wrote Kathryn enthusiastically about the beauty of Bedford Park, and in his articles for the *Boston Pilot* throughout 1890 and 1891 he consistently praised it for being a colony of writers and artists and gave a general impression of positive identification with the place. But perhaps more important than this was the apparent willingness of the other residents to accept Willy for what he was —every inch a poet—as this article in the Acton paper indicates.

Mr. W. B. Yeats, who meditates publishing at once a volume of his poems, is, says the *Morning Leader*, one of the most popular members of the Metropolitan literary gatherings. He still lives at his father's house at Bedford Park, where, by the way, he has a delightful study. It opens out on a miniature balcony, and—inasmuch as he is passionately fond of flowers—he usually has one or two choice blossoms growing there. Disturb them and you arouse at once his most violent animosity. His appearance is half-poetic, half masculine. He has the poet's forehead, and in moments of irritation or emotion he will sweep the dusky hair from off it. The chin is, however, firm and reliant, and the mouth is close set with an air of strong determination. . . . Yet withal he is somewhat a literary dandy. He used to affect carelessly tied red ties; he wears a picturesque soft hat, and he introduces cadences—true, they are very rich—into his conversation. He is a striking looking fellow. He is tall and lath-like; His face is as dark as Mr. Naoroji's—it is long and oval, and from out it gaze two large sad brown eyes.[2]

Yeats was certainly not stifled by Bedford Park; he practiced his art unhindered by philistines, and in his work with other residents at the club theater he learned something useful about his craft. In retrospect he admitted that what he

116

learned about the theater while helping Todhunter produce *The Sicilian Idyll* had a profound influence on his later aims for The Irish Theatre. His own experience bears out the success of the community. Perhaps Yeats, in his fame, is the exception that proved the rule. It is noteworthy that the Irish Literary Revival was born at the Yeats house at a meeting called by Willy on 28 December 1891, and the house was described by one of the participants, W. P. Ryan, as "in every sense a meet haunt for a poet or an artist."[3]

G. K. Chesterton's attitude toward Bedford Park is analagous to Yeats's in its combination of respect and ridicule. He recreates it as Saffron Park, a neighborhood of political crackpots in *The Man Who Was Thursday*, drawing on the reputation for socialism and nihilism that the presence of Sergius Stepniak and a few milder socialists like York Powell and R. A. M. Stevenson had given the place. His own participation in political discussions there, particularly during the Boer War, may have added to the radical reputation of the Park, for Chesterton was pro-Boer and a willing combatant in the frequent meetings held there to "discuss" the role of the British Empire in South Africa. He was a frequent visitor because he was long courting a resident whom he eventually married, Frances Blogg.

In his autobiography, Chesterton notes that Bedford Park, so strikingly unusual to begin with from an architectural point of view, had by 1936 so far merged with the rest of London that it had become hard to remember how odd it had appeared in the beginning. He felt that in a sense Bedford Park had "conquered" the rest of the world because the picturesque red brick style had come into such common use for all kinds of buildings. He felt that although there was something slightly theatrical about the intellectual pretensions of the place there were indeed some intelligent people

117

living there, that it was not a fraud, and it is interesting that he thinks of William Butler Yeats in this connection:

> . . . If it was a place of shadows it could hardly be called a place of shams, when it contained one who is still perhaps the greatest poet writing in our tongue. There is always something fanciful about the conjunction of the world that the poet sees and the place he lives in. . . . And it amuses me to think that under those toy trees and gimcrack gables there was already passing a pageant of strange gods and the head-dresses of forgotten priests and the horns of holy unicorns and the wrinkled sleep of Druidic vegetation, and all the emblems of a new heraldry of the human imagination.[4]

The general feeling in Chesterton's memories of Bedford Park is one of fondness, with a tinge of criticism. However, it is obvious from his account that he thought the community worked in the way that its founders intended it to. People who lived there gave something to the community and got from it in return a sense of identity that they valued. The whole was greater than the individual parts.

BEDFORD PARK THROUGH THE YEARS

Although the sense of community which could generate a workable forum like the Bedford Park Committee and support a newspaper like the *Bedford Park Gazette* was showing signs of disintegration as early as 1884, the community in a larger sense lasted for many years and, in fact, in a highly modified form is present today, for it continues to be a pleasant place to live and the present residents claim to feel a community spirit there which they have not felt in other places. Their efforts to preserve Bedford Park are evidence of that feeling.

Information about life in Bedford Park between the end of the nineteenth century and 1967 is sketchy. When the residents of surrounding neighborhoods became accustomed to the Bedford Park community and the rest of the world started building in Queen Anne style, the local newspapers stopped paying so much attention to what went on in Bedford Park. As Chesterton observed, the world got to be so much like Bedford Park it was not an oddity. But an advertisement for new members for the club in the *Brentford and Chiswick Times*, 7 April 1933, indicates that it was still the center of life in the community and the scene of continued activity for some of the societies which had been organized by 1884. The Tennis Club, Dramatic Society, and Gardening Society were still active, as well as a newer Bridge Club. It is interesting that at this time the club was enjoying the tenure of only its second president, Sir Thomas Edwards Forster, who had succeeded J. T. Carr. The Bedford Park Club ceased to exist in 1939 when the practical difficulties of running it in a wartime economy made it unfeasible. The building and fittings were sold at public auction. It is now a private club. The church, Saint Michael and All Angels, and the pub, the Tabard, still serve their original functions. The School of Art has become the Chiswick Polytechnic. In fact, according to T. A. Greeves, all the public buildings remain in pretty much their original external form except the School of Art, and most of the houses designed by Godwin and Shaw still exist although many have lost their original architectural features.

In 1963 The Bedford Park Society was formed under the patronage of Sir John Betjeman with the principal aim of getting the Ministry of Housing to declare Bedford Park an area of special architectural and historic interest. In 1967, 350 houses were provisionally put on the ministry's Grade Two list of historic buildings, which means that none can be altered or redeveloped without the ministry's permission. The justification for requesting that Bedford Park be listed and therefore preserved is interesting for the light shed on the appeal of the community at the present time. T. A. Greeves, the writer of the following plea, is an architect and authority on Bedford Park who was deeply involved in the campaign which succeeded in getting Bedford Park listed.

> Bedford Park must be preserved for three reasons: Firstly, it can claim to be the first garden suburb by virtue of its tree-conscious layout, and its public buildings, which made it a self-contained residential unit, with a social emphasis on art; in this sense it is more complete than Hampstead Garden Suburb, the first estate to which that term was applied, which was begun thirty years later. Secondly, the architectural ideas first expressed here can be found in one form or another in Bourneville, Port Sunlight (listed by the Ministry), Letchworth, Hampstead (listed by the Ministry) and Welwyn, all built later than Bedford Park, the elimination of the basement being its main planning contribution. Thirdly, its attractive and sensibly planned houses, in an area of comparatively high density, form a compact residential enclave with an architectural quality and a rural atmosphere without parallel in inner suburban London. The transport facilities which so attracted Carr are even better today. The houses are mostly not too large for family houses, the attics being readily convertible into playrooms or studios. A number of houses have studios in their gardens, built for the numerous artists who originally lived here, and now used by their successors. Some of the larger houses have been successfully converted into flats or maisonettes, and their sound construction can be attested to by the fact that even after the ninety or so years since they were built almost all of them still survive, many with their original attractive tiled fireplaces.[5]

So Bedford Park has survived and prevailed. The community spirit which it still generates led to the Bedford Park Society's sponsoring a Bedford Park Festival in 1967 which included an architectural exhibit, architectural tours of the community, an art show of work done by early residents, and an exhibition of furniture such as that used by early residents. Another fête was held in 1971, and the Bedford Park Centenary was celebrated in 1975 to coincide with European Architectural Heritage Year. It is interesting that one of the cohesive forces in the present community is Bedford Park's heritage. The past has become a source of pride for the present.

APPENDIX A

THE BALLAD OF BEDFORD PARK

In London town there lived a man
    a gentleman was he
Whose name was Jonathan T. Carr
    (as has been told to me).

"This London is a foggy town"
    (thus to himself said he),
"Where bricks are black, and trees are brown
    and faces are dirtee.

"I will seek out a brighter spot,"
    continued Mr. Carr.
"Not too near London, and yet not
    what might be called too far.

"'Tis there a village I'll erect
    with Norman Shaw's assistance
Where men may lead a chaste correct
    aesthetical existence."

With that a passing 'bus he hailed
    (so gallant to be seen)
Upon whose knife-board he did ride
    as far as Turnham Green.

"Oh, here we are," said Mr. Carr.
    "No further will I roam;
This is the spot that fate has got
    to give us for our home.

"'Tis here, my Norman, tried and true,
    our houses we'll erect;
I'll be the landlord bold, and you
    shall be the architect.

"Here trees are green and bricks are red
    and clean the face of man.
We'll build our houses here," he said
    "in style of good Queen Anne."

And Norman Shaw looked up and saw,
    and smiled a cheerful smile.
"This thing I'll do, said he, "while you
    the denizens beguile."

To work went then, these worthy men,
    so philanthropic both.
And none who sees the bricks and trees
    to sign the lease is loth.

"Let's have a store," said Jonathan.
    Said Norman, "So we will,
For nought can soothe the soul of man
    like a reasonable bill."

"A Church likewise," J. T. replies.
      Says Shaw, "I'll build a Church,
Yet sore, I fear, the aesthetes here
      will leave it in the lurch."

"Religion," pious Carr rejoined,
      "in Mon-Cure Conway's view,
Is not devoid of interest
      although it be not true.

"Then let us make a house for her,
      where in she may abide,
And those who choose may visit her,
      the rest may stay outside.

"But lest the latter should repine
      a tennis ground we'll make
Where they on Sunday afternoons
      may recreation take."

Then each t'other winked his eye
      and next they did prepare
A noble Clubhouse to supply
      with decorations fair.

With red and blue and sagest green
      were walls and dado dyed,
Friezes of Morris there were seen
      and oaken wainscot wide.

Thus was a village builded
      for all who are aesthete
Whose precious souls it fill did
      with utter joy complete.

For floors were stained and polished
     and every hearth was tiled
And Philistines abolished
     by Culture's gracious child.

And Abbey (he the artist,
     malicious little wretch)
Said it made him feel like walking
     through a water-colour sketch.

And Jonathan and Norman
     found so much work to do,
They sold out to a Company
     to put the business through.

Now he who loves aesthetic cheer
     and does not mind the damp
May come and read Rossetti here
     by a Japanese-y lamp.

While "Arry" shouts to "Hemmua":
     "Say, 'ere's a bloomin' lark,
Thems the biled Lobster 'ouses
     as folks calls 'Bedford Park.' "[1]

APPENDIX B

"DISTINCTLY PRECIOUS PANTOMIME"

Dear Mr. Punch,

A letter from "an old clown" which recently appeared in your Contemporary is all nonsense. Clowns, if they wish to keep their place upon the stage, must go with the times. They must become aesthetic. A long-haired clown, a flabby harlequin, an intense Pantaloon, and a Burnes-Jonesian Columbine, would be a great success. Fancy a lugubrious clown singing the following version of

HOT CODLINS

Some foolish young people, quite famous
    they got
By posing, and talking—rot, rot, rot!
They made themselves Guys, not fit to
    be seen,
and painted their walls a sad, sage
    green;
They worshipped in silence their white
    and blue,
and their friends all said they were
    quite ——— ———.

Da-do, daffodilly, silly-billy
Sunflower, Botticelli, quite
too-too!
These foolish young people, they cared
not a jot;
They thought they knew what was what,
what, what!
They painted poems they averred were good;
They sang sweet pictures that none
understood.
And though it was said they had no common
sense,
Everyone declared they were much too ———.
Da-do, daffodilly, silly-billy,
Sunflower, Botticelli, quite too-too!

Would not that be splendid? I may inform you, in the strictest confidence, that Mr. E. L. Blanchard is going to write, for the Drury Lane Annual next season, *Harlequin Dado and the Sighing Sunflower*; or *The Languorous Lilies of Limpshire*, in which there will doubtless be an ample field for the display of the talents of
Your obedient Servant
A Young Clown[1]

Bedford Park

NOTES

INTRODUCTION

1. Lewis Mumford, *The City in History* (New York, 1961), pp. 482–83.
2. Eric E. Lampard, "The Urbanizing World," in *The Victorian City*, ed. J. J. Dyos and Michael Wolff (London and Boston, 1973), 1:4.
3. H. J. Dyos and D. A. Reeder, "Slums and Suburbs," in *The Victorian City*, 1:326.
4. Charles Dickens. *Bleak House* (New York, 1970), p. 1.
5. H. G. Wells, *Experiment in Autobiography* (London, 1934), p. 224.

CHAPTER 1

1. Walter L. Creese, "The Oasis at Bedford Park," *The Search for Environment* (New Haven, 1966), pp. 87–107; Ian Fletcher, "Bedford Park Aesthete's Elysium?" in *Romantic Mythologies*, ed. Ian Fletcher (London, 1967), pp. 169–207; Mark Glazebrook, "Some Artists of Bedford Park 1877–1900," in *Artists and Architecture of Bedford Park 1875–1900*, ed. Mark Glazebrook (London, 1967), pp. 9–48; T. Affleck Greeves, "Brief Architectural History of Bedford Park," in *Artists and Architects of Bedford Park 1875–1900*, pp. 49–62; and "London's First Garden Suburb," *Country Life*, 7 and 14 December 1967.
2. John Betjeman, "Suburbs Common or Garden," *Daily Telegraph and Morning News*, 22 August 1960.
3. *Bedford Park Gazette*, August 1883, p. 17.
4. *Harper's New Monthly Magazine*, March 1881, pp. 481-490.
5. Ellen Conway to Mr. Harrison, The Conway Collection, Columbia University Library.
6. H. S. Goodhart-Rendel, *English Architecture since the Regency* (London, 1953), p. 153.

7. William Butler Yeats, *Autobiographies* (London, 1926), p. 166.

8. Reginald Blomfield, *Richard Norman Shaw, R. A.* (London, 1940), pp. 34-36 (see Appendix A of this book for complete poem).

9. E. V. Lucas, *Edwin Austin Abbey Royal Academician* (London, 1921), 1:84.

CHAPTER 2

1. *Bedford Park Gazette*, July 1883.

2. Eve Adams, ed., *Mrs. J. Comyns Carr's Reminiscences* (London, 1925), p. 27.

3. *Chiswick Times*, 5 February 1915.

4. *Building News*, 22 December 1876. There are inaccuracies of detail in this account. As Greeves points out, most of the houses were built of local red brick with walls 13½ inches thick on plots with average frontage of thirty feet. Only two of Godwin's plans were used (T. Affleck Greeves, "Brief Architectural History of Bedford Park," in *Artists and Architects of Bedford Park 1875-1900*, ed. Mark Glazebrook [London, 1967], p. 50).

5. *Building News*, 2 February 1877.

6. Walter L. Creese, "The Oasis at Bedford Park," *The Search for Environment* (New Haven, 1966), p. 98.

7. *Building News*, 9 February 1877.

8. Ibid., 23 November 1877.

9. Ibid., 9 February 1877.

10. Ibid., 9 November 1877.

11. Moncure Conway, "Bedford Park," *Harper's New Monthly Magazine*, March 1881, p. 489.

12. *Bedford Park Gazette*, July 1883.

13. Greeves, "Brief Architectural History," p. 56.

14. Ibid.

15. *The Pioneer*, 22 March 1881, p. 1.

16. Conway, "Bedford Park," p. 484.

17. Greeves, "Brief Architectural History," p. 54.

18. "An Artist's House, C. F. A. Voysey, Architect," *The British Architect*, September 1891, p. 209.

19. C. F. A. Voysey, *Individuality* (London, 1915), p. 86.

20. Powell to Ker, 18 January 1892, in Oliver Elton, *Frederick York Powell* (Oxford, 1906), 1:139.

21. Conway, "Bedford Park," p. 483.

22. "Bedford Park, London," *Chambers's Journal*, 31 December 1881, p. 41.

23. *Acton and Chiswick Gazette*, 15 June 1895, p. 6.

CHAPTER 3

1. *Acton, Chiswick & Turnham Green Gazette*, 2 July 1887.
2. *Punch*, 17 September 1878.
3. *Acton, Chiswick & Turnham Green Gazette*, 3 February 1883.
4. Moncure Daniel Conway, "The Gospel of Art," *Addresses and Reprints* (Boston, 1909), p. 255.
5. *Acton, Chiswick & Turnham Green Gazette*, 17 April 1880.
6. William Butler Yeats, *Autobiographies* (London, 1955), p. 43.
7. Oliver Elton, *Frederick York Powell* (Oxford, 1906), 1:63.
8. *Bedford Park Gazette*, July 1883.
9. *Acton, Chiswick & Turnham Green Gazette*, 18 November 1880.
10. *The Bedford Park Gazette*, July 1883.
11. Ibid., October 1883.
12. Ibid., July 1883.
13. Walter Hamilton, *The Aesthetic Movement in England* (London, 1882), p. 121.
14. *Acton, Chiswick & Turnham Green Gazette*, 2 November 1895.
15. Powell to Elton, 31 January 1892, in Elton, *York Powell*, 1:140.
16. *Dictionary of National Biography*, s.v. "Powell, Frederick York."
17. Powell to Vigfusson, 18 August 1882, in Elton, *York Powell* 1:67.
18. Powell to Ker, 2 February 1889, in ibid., 1:63.
19. *Bedford Park Gazette*, July 1883.
20. Ibid., September 1883.
21. Ibid., November 1883.

CHAPTER 4

1. *Bedford Park Gazette*, September 1883.
2. Ian Fletcher, "Bedford Park, Aesthete's Elysium?" in *Romantic Mythologies* (London, 1967), p. 170.
3. Moncure Daniel Conway, "Bedford Park," *Harper's New Monthly Magazine*, March 1881, p. 489.
4. *Bedford Park Gazette*, December 1883.
5. Ibid., July 1883.
6. Ibid., October 1883.
7. Ibid., February 1884.
8. Ibid., July 1884.
9. *Acton and Chiswick Gazette*, 13 July 1895.

10. Conway, "Bedford Park," p. 486.

11. *Acton, Chiswick & Turnham Green Gazette*, 4 March, 1882.

12. Ibid.

13. *Bedford Park Gazette*, January, 1884.

14. Moncure Daniel Conway, *Autobiography*, II, p. 488.

15. *Bedford Park Gazette*, July, 1883.

16. Ibid., July, 1883.

17. Conway, "Bedford Park," p. 487.

18. *Boston Daily Advertiser*, 8 July 1880.

19. A. H. Huth, *On the Employment of Women* (London, 1882), p. 14.

20. Thomas Barrett Lennard, *The Position in Law of Women* (London, 1883), p. 1.

21. *Acton, Chiswick & Turnham Green Gazette*, 10 June 1882.

22. Viscountess Harberton (Florence Pomeroy), *Reasons for Reform in Dress* (London, 1885), p. 17.

23. *Acton, Chiswick & Turnham Green Gazette*, 2 December 1882.

24. *Acton, Chiswick & Turnham Green Gazette*, 9 June, 1883.

25. Ibid., 9 June 1883.

26. Ibid., 9 June 1883.

27. *The Whitehall Review*, 24 October 1883.

28. *Acton, Chiswick & Turnham Green Gazette*, 20 December 1884.

29. *Bedford Park Gazette*, June 1884.

30. Ibid.

31. Ibid., July, 1884.

32. *Acton, Chiswick & Turnham Green Gazette*, 6 July 1895.

33. G. K. Chesterton, *Autobiography* (London, 1936), p. 141.

34. John Butler Yeats to ——, ——, in Yeats, *Letters to His Son W. B. Yeats and Others*, ed. Joseph Hone (London, 1944), p. 325.

35. Conway, *Autobiography*, p. 325.

36. William Butler Yeats, *Letters to a New Island* (Cambridge, 1934), p. 105.

37. Ibid., p. 114.

38. William Butler Yeats, *Autobiographies* (London, 1926), p. 148.

39. William Butler Yeats, "The Theatre," reprinted in *Essays and Introductions* (New York, 1968), p. 166.

40. Clifford Bax, ed., *Florence Farr, Bernard Shaw, W. B. Yeats Letters* (New York, 1942), p. 48.

41. *Acton, Chiswick & Turnham Green Gazette*, 28 May 1880.

42. *Bedford Park Gazette*, July 1883.

43. I am indebted to Mr. R. B. Unwin for this information. Mr. Unwin was born in Bedford Park in 1888 and lived there until 1915.

44. *Bedford Park Gazette*, November 1883.

45. *Acton and Chiswick Gazette*, 2 January 1892.

46. Ibid., 10 January 1896.

47. Ibid., 14 August 1880.

CHAPTER 5

1. Yeats to Tynan, 5 March, in W. B. Yeats, *Letters to Kathryn Tynan* (New York, 1952), p. 48.

2. *Acton and Chiswick Gazette*, 27 April 1895.

3. W. P. Ryan, *The Irish Literary Revival* (London, 1894), p. 52.

4. G. K. Chesterton, *Autobiography* (New York, 1936), p. 139.

5. T. Affleck Greeves, "Brief Architectural History of Bedford Park," in *Artists and Architects of Bedford Park 1875-1900* (London, 1967), p. 62.

APPENDIX A

1. Reginald Blomfield, *Richard Norman Shaw, R. A.* (London, 1940), pp. 34-36.

APPENDIX B

1. *Punch*, 4 February 1882, p. 49.

INDEX